Cambridge Business English Activities

Serious fun for Business English students

Jane Cordell

CAMBRIDGE
UNIVERSITY PRESS

PUBLISHED BY THE PRESS SYNDICATE OF THE UNIVERSITY OF CAMBRIDGE
The Pitt Building, Trumpington Street, Cambridge, United Kingdom

CAMBRIDGE UNIVERSITY PRESS
The Edinburgh Building, Cambridge CB2 2RU, UK
40 West 20th Street, New York, NY 10011–4211, USA
477 Williamstown Road, Port Melbourne, VIC 3207, Australia
Ruiz de Alarcón 13, 28014 Madrid, Spain
Dock House, The Waterfront, Cape Town 8001, South Africa

http://www.cambridge.org

First published 2000
Third printing 2003

Printed in the United Kingdom at the University Press, Cambridge

ISBN 0521 58734 4

Thanks and acknowledgements

This book is dedicated to the business English group at ABB Zamech Ltd in Elbląg, Poland, 1993–4. I would like to thank them for providing the inspiration for many of the activities in this book and for their enthusiasm and patience as my guinea pigs.

I have been incredibly lucky to have the support of a number of people whilst writing this book, so would like to thank Sarah Almy for her vision, limitless patience, clear and practical guidance and encouragement; to Tina Ottman for her good humoured and careful copy editing; to Jayshree Ramsurun for taking the book through pilot stage and for keeping the project well on course; to Sally Searby for steering the book safely through to publication; to Olive and Jim Cordell for unstinting practical advice, support and love and to Sean Cordell and Helen Krawczyk for advice on culinary matters; finally to Colin Bagnall for his inspired artistic work with the group mentioned above when he visited us in Poland.

Thanks and acknowledgements are also due for the following activities:

Intonation dictation

This activity is inspired by an introduction to teaching intonation given during my initial training by the wonderful teacher, Martin Parrott.

Testing each other

This activity is based on a favourite teaching technique of my stalwart colleague at the College of North West London, Richard Oakes. I thank him both for this idea and for many other useful ones.

The author and publishers would like to thank the following individuals and institutions for their help in piloting and commenting on the material and for the invaluable feedback which they provided:

Maria Cristina Brieba, Instituto Chileno Británico, Santiago, Chile; Moira Hotz-Hart, Swiss Telecom, Bolligen, Switzerland; Veronica Lee, British Council, Hong Kong; Glen Penrod, Samsung Human Resources Development Center, Korea; Jane Ross, Korean Register of Shipping, Daejeon, Korea; Tess Pacey, International House, Paris, France; Roy Gooding, Centum, Buenos Aires, Argentina; Professor Suchada Nimmannit, Chulalongkorn University, Bangkok, Thailand; John Crowther-Alwyn, Assimilation, France; Angela Winkler, Germany; Nicky Pierre, Germany; Jioanna Carjuzaa, University Of Pennsylvania, USA; Carolyn Heard, Martha Bordman, Joan Friedman, American Language Institute, New York University, USA; Kevin McNally, Hampstead School of English, UK.

The author and publishers are grateful to the following photographic Sources: Burgum Boorman, V.C.L/Nick Clements, Digital Vision, Richard Radstone, Stephen Simpson, and Nick White.

Map of the book

Introduction, p8

Activity and page number	Level	Business/ social function	Language focus	Timing	Type of activity	One-to-one
Unit 1: Finding out about your students						
1.1 Four skills needs analysis p9	Lower-intermediate	Discussing English language needs	Asking questions	30–40 minutes	Groups of four	Possible if adapted
1.2 This is me p12	Intermediate (adaptable for other levels)	Describing yourself	Adjectives and their antonyms	40 minutes	Individual then group	Yes
1.3 Graph skills analysis p14	Lower-intermediate	Describing English ability	Modals of ability	35–45 minutes	Individual and small groups	Yes
1.4 Personality scales p16	Mid-intermediate	Getting to know someone	Second conditional	50–55 minutes	Pair	Yes
1.5 Identity swap p19	Lower-intermediate	Finding out about new people	Question forms	30–40 minutes	Whole class	No
Unit 2: Socializing in English						
2.1 Introducing yourself and others p20	Lower-intermediate	Formal introduction and polite interruption	Polite greetings and question tags at higher levels	10–30 minutes (depending on level)	Whole class	Possible if adapted
2.2 Restaurant board game p23	Lower-intermediate	Socializing at a business lunch	Polite requests, enquiries and suggestions	70–90 minutes	Small group	Possible if adapted
2.3 Question and answer Pelmanism p28	Pre-/Mid-intermediate	Recognizing common social exchanges	Basic social questions and answers	12–15 minutes	Pairs and small groups	Yes
2.4 Asking questions p30	Elementary, pre-intermediate	Asking basic questions	Question forms	35–35 minutes	Class and pair	Yes

Unit 3: Using the phone

3.1 A telephone maze p33	Mid-intermediate	Telephoning	Enquiring and checking	30–35 minutes	Class and pair	Yes
3.2 Phone quartets p36	Lower-intermediate	Telephoning for a variety of purposes	Telephone language	40–60 minutes	Groups of four	No
3.3 What not to do p39	Intermediate	Dealing with angry and impolite callers	Rude and tactful language on the phone	20–40 minutes	Cross-class pairs	Yes

Unit 4: Business writing

4.1 Formal or informal? p41	Intermediate/upper-intermediate	Recognizing register in letters	Letter language/register	30 minutes	Pairs or threes	Yes
4.2 Writing a CV p45	Lower-intermediate	Discussing someone's experience	Past simple and present perfect questions; time prepositions	35–60 minutes	Pair	Yes
4.3 A letter to correct p47	Intermediate/upper-intermediate	Recognizing errors in a business letter	Error correction	30–45 minutes	Pair	Yes
4.4 A group letter p50	Lower-/upper-intermediate	Organizing a business letter	Using conjunctions	12 minutes or 22–37 minutes with extension activity	Whole class	Possible if adapted
4.5 Keeping it brief p53	Elementary intermediate Upper-intermediate	Writing a memo/fax after scan and skim reading	Language of faxes and memos	E 75–90 minutes; I/U 45–75 minutes	Individual and pairs	Yes

Unit 5: Making decisions

5.1 Bingo diaries p58	Lower-intermediate	Arranging times to meet	Time expressions with present continuous	20–30 minutes	Small group	Possible if adapted
5.2 Napoleon's decision-making p64	Upper-Intermediate	Reaching a decision	Agreeing and disagreeing; giving and discussing opinions	30–60 minutes	Individuals, pairs and fours	Possible if adapted

5.3 How shall we market it? p67	Mid-intermediate Intermediate Advanced	Discussing how to market a product	Agreeing, disagreeing and reaching a group decision	75–90 minutes	Small group	Possible if adapted
5.4 A meeting p71	Upper-intermediate	Holding a meeting	Agreeing, disagreeing, asking for and giving opinions	60 minutes	Group	Possible if adapted
Unit 6: Negotiating						
6.1 Conditionals in a negotiation p73	Upper-intermediate	Negotiating	First and second conditionals	30 minutes	Whole class	Yes
6.2 Someone else's shoes p75	Mid-intermediate	Recognizing the other party's position in a negotiation	The language of negotiating	60–80 minutes	Pair	Yes
Unit 7: Describing change						
7.1 The crystal ball game p80	Lower-intermediate	Predicting future changes	Will/ going to	20–40 minutes depending on size of class	Whole class	Possible if adapted
7.2 A company's progress p81	Intermediate Upper-intermediate	Describing a company's development	The language of change	30 minutes	Small group and pair	Yes
7.3 Graph dictations p84	Lower-intermediate	Describing a line graph	The language of change	35–45 minutes	Pair	Yes
Unit 8: Describing companies and jobs						
8.1 Describe an organigram p87	Intermediate+	Describing company structure	Position, relative position	50–80 minutes	Whole class	Yes
8.2 Talking pictures p88	Intermediate	Describing and speculating	Agreeing and disagreeing plus modals	30–40 minutes	Pairs and threes	Possible if adapted
8.3 My working day p91	Elementary	Describing a work routine	Modals of possibility	35–55 minutes	Pairs	Yes
Unit 9: Describing processes						
9.1 A roof over your head? p93	Upper-intermediate	Organizing a process description	Instructions	45–60 minutes	Whole class and group	Yes
9.2 The process jigsaw p95	Mid-intermediate	Marking the stages of a process with key words	Cohesive and referential words	85–120 minutes	Pair	Possible if adapted

Unit 10: Making comparisons

10.1 The best offer p99	Lower-Upper-intermediate	Agreeing, disagreeing and persuading	Comparatives and superlatives	60–80 minutes	Small group	Possible if adapted
10.2 Selling yourself p103	Pre-intermediate Intermediate	Describing yourself and preparing for interview	Comparatives and superlatives	30–40 minutes	Individual and pair	Yes

Unit 11: Pronunciation

11.1 Intonation patterns p105	All	Appreciating the effects of different intonation		20–30 minutes	Pair	Yes
11.2 A phonemic phone call p107	Intermediate	Recognizing the order of a business call	The IPA	20–30 minutes	Pair or whole class	Possible if adapted
11.3 Strong or weak? p109	Intermediate	Recognizing weak forms	Describing a procedure	45 minutes	Threes	Yes

Unit 12: Giving feedback to your students

12.1 A memo to your students p113	Any	Giving feedback	Depends on language used by students	15–20 minutes	Individual and group	Yes
12.2 Pairs to compare p116	Any	Error recognition	Depends on language by students	10–20 minutes	Pairs	Yes

Unit 13: Giving advice

13.1 When it goes wrong p117	Pre-intermediate	Giving advice	Advice modals	45 minutes	Whole group writing	Possible if adapted
13.2 Business scruples p118	Mid-intermediate	Expressing opinions and giving advice	'If I were you ...' and advice modals	40–65 minutes	Small group	Yes

Unit 14: Using numbers

14.1 Number noughts and crosses p120	Intermediate+	Using variety of numbers	Numbers	20–25 minutes	Pair	Possible if adapted
14.2 Checking the details p122	Pre-intermediate	Using variety of numbers	Numbers and using contrastive stress	15–25 minutes	Pair or teacher-led whole class	Yes
14.3 Shared number dictations p124	Intermediate	Using variety of numbers	Numbers	20–30 minutes	Pair	Yes
14.4 Testing each other p128	Pre-intermediate	Using variety of numbers	Numbers and using contrastive stress	15–25 minutes	Pair or teacher-led whole class	Yes

Introduction

Welcome to *Cambridge Business English Activities!* I hope that you will enjoy using it with your students.

What is *Cambridge Business English Activities*?

Cambridge Business English Activities is a book of 43 activities for enlivening business English classes. The activities are student-centred, highly participative and designed to complement most business English syllabi and coursebooks. As many of the activities are designed to provide students with conversation practice, they can also be used successfully with students of general English.

Who is the book for?

The book can be used with both experienced business people and pre-experience learners, in a variety of learning contexts. It has been designed as a flexible resource. There are whole group, small group and pairwork activities, with information in the **Teaching notes** on adapting the material for different-sized groups. Using it in a one-to-one situation is also given special comment. Almost all the activities can be used with a micro group or in a one-to-one class.

Which levels can the material be used with?

There are activities for elementary up to advanced levels in this book and the **Teaching notes** for each activity indicate the most appropriate level(s) for use. The activities foster a cooperative approach to learning that can help mixed level groups work better together. Also, the **Teaching notes** indicate when an activity can be adapted easily to other levels.

Using the activities

The **Map of the book** has been divided into sections under functional headings similar to those used in many business English coursebooks so that the activities can be used alongside such books.

The **Teaching notes** for each activity provide a clear, step-by-step description of how to carry out that activity in class, and there is a section which describes any pre-class preparation needed. Suggestions are made as to how to give feedback and, where appropriate, how to follow up the activity.

As this material is designed to be as flexible as possible, a precise list of language components is not provided for each activity. However, an indication is made at the start of the notes of which language areas will be practised. The actual language used by each group of students will depend on their ability, and, to some extent, the language you choose to emphasize.

A **Map of the book** follows this introduction, giving a complete breakdown of each activity. This will be particularly useful for teachers who need to select an activity very quickly.

Class management

Many of the activities in the book require the focus to be placed on the students. Be prepared to change your own position, and occasionally, to rearrange the classroom or training room to facilitate this. Ask yourself where you can stand or sit so that the students do not always feel obliged to acknowledge your presence. Also, how can the furniture be best positioned to allow for good communication, and if necessary, group changes? Initially you may find your students resistant to any sort of change in the classroom hierarchy or system, but a little physical movement in class can be very energizing and, once encouraged, most students see the benefits it can bring.

Facilities

The material in this book marked © **Cambridge University Press 2000** `PHOTOCOPIABLE` may be reproduced and can be used in any classroom with a blackboard or a whiteboard. For some activities, however, an OHP or flip-chart will enhance a particular stage of a lesson and where this is the case, advice is given in the **Teaching notes**. If possible, use the walls of the room in which you teach to display students' work or the results of some of the activities (e.g. the **Four skills needs analysis** chart, or **Graph skills analysis** results). If you have access to a cassette recorder and/ or video camera and VCR, you could think about using them to provide feedback.

Giving feedback

Each teacher has his/her own methods for observing students' language and providing feedback on it. But if you need a few more ideas, there are two activities in the final section of the book called **Giving feedback** that you might like to try, and many of the activities also have a feedback stage described. Videoing or recording your students, with their prior permission of course, is a stimulating and revealing way of gathering information and means that students can participate in analyzing good use of language and their own errors.

Finally, I would be delighted to get feedback from you, the teachers using the material. Please write to me at the publisher if you have any comments to make.

1.1 Four skills needs analysis

Teaching notes

To practise Asking questions, discussing English language needs and presenting information.

Level Lower-intermediate and above.

Class size Ideally four students or multiples of four. If you have one extra student, s/he should pair up with another student and share a question card. With two or three extra students, they can double up their cards.

Pre-experience learners This is an activity aimed at those students who already have some business experience and wish to use their English at work.

However, you could redesign the cards using more general categories for pre-experience learners.

One-to-one Not ideal, but teacher and student can analyze the student's marks, using them as a basis for discussing the student's needs and possibly also for devising a course syllabus.

Timing 30–40 minutes.

You will need One copy of each of the **Worksheets** (p10–11), cut into four, per group of four students. A flipchart is an advantage for stage four.

Procedure

You can use this activity early on in a course to work out a course syllabus which matches, as far as possible, your students' needs.

1. Explain to students that they are going to do some research to find out what they need to do most in English. Put students into groups of four, or as close as possible to this. Tell them that each of them will research one of the main study skills. Hand out a different section of the **Worksheet** to each member of each group and ask students first to complete the column headed 'Me' for themselves. If necessary, you could demonstrate this using one student's answers.

2. Next, students interview colleagues in their group about their needs and fill in the remaining columns. Encourage pairs to work at a similar pace where possible. Discuss answers with any students who are waiting to interview an occupied student.

3. When everyone has been interviewed, ask students to add up the horizontal total for each item on their worksheet and write it in the 'Total' column. They should then highlight the items with the highest scores. One representative for each group should then collate this information. While students are doing this, put the four skills as headings on a flipchart, if possible, or if not, on the board.

4. Starting with one skill, e.g. reading, ask each group representative in turn to report on the things their group needs to be able to do most. Where an item is repeated, add a tick or star to it. Then go through the other skills in the same way.

5. The teacher or a confident volunteer then presents the collated class material.

Follow up

Note down the information from this class and produce a poster with a heading such as 'Our class priorities' for the wall, or make a handout.

Periodically, check whether the list is still relevant to your students and revise it as appropriate.

A Reading

How important is it for you to be able to read these things in English? Mark each one from 1 (not important/never do it) to 5 (very important/I really need to be able to do this) in the 'Me' column. Then ask the other students in your group and put their marks in the other columns.

	Me	Student 1	Student 2	Student 3	Total
Business letters					
Reports and memos					
Faxes					
Newspapers and magazines					
Specialist journals					
Marketing and publicity material					
Books connected with your work					
Reference material (e.g. trade directories)					
Other?					

B Listening

How important is it for you to be able to listen to and understand these things in English? Mark each one from 1 (not important/never do it) to 5 (very important/I really need to be able to do this) in the 'Me' column. Then ask the other students in your group and put their marks in the other columns.

	Me	Student 1	Student 2	Student 3	Total
Presentations					
People speaking on the phone					
People speaking at meetings					
Lectures					
Social talk					
TV programmes and videos					
Radio					
Recorded material, e.g. answerphone, voice mail					
Other?					

C Writing

How important is it for you to be able to write these things in English? Mark each one from 1 (unimportant/I never do it) to 5 (very important/I really need to be able to do this) in the 'Me' column. Then ask the other students in your group and put their marks in the other columns.

	Me	Student 1	Student 2	Student 3	Total
Business letters					
Faxes					
Short messages, notes and memos					
Articles					
Reports					
Notes for presentations					
Formal speeches					
Other?					

D Speaking

How important is it for you to be able to do these things in English? Mark each one from 1 (not important/I never do it) to 5 (very important/I really need to be able to do this) in the 'Me' column. Then interview the other students in your group and fill in their answers in the other columns.

	Me	Student 1	Student 2	Student 3	Total
Speak on the phone					
Speak face to face in business meetings					
Speak face to face in social situations					
Negotiate					
Give a presentation					
Give a formal speech					
Give a lecture					
Sell or promote a product or service					
Discuss statistics					
Show visitors around					
Other?					

1.2 This is me

Teaching notes

To practise Using adjectives and their antonyms to describe feelings and personality in the present continuous and simple tenses.

Level Intermediate, but easily adapted to other levels with different lists of words.

Pre-experience learners No special preparation needed.

Class size Four or more works best. With large classes of ten plus, provide double copies of the words.

One-to-one You could lay the words out on the table rather than putting them on the walls, but the walking around can energize and/or break the ice.

Overall timing 40 minutes.

You will need Copies of the worksheet **Words to describe ourselves** (p13) for each member of class. Stickers or small cards in two colours. Write one word from column A or B (see worksheet) on each card or sticker (use one colour for column A words, and another colour for column B words). Write each word once only.

Procedure

1 Prepare the classroom, before the lesson if possible, by putting the words around the walls. Mix up the words; no special order is needed.

2 Tell students that they are going to find out more about each other. Write two questions on the board: 'How are you feeling now?' and 'What are you like?'. Check with a few brief answers that students understand the difference between the latter question and 'What do you like?'.

3 Indicate the words on the walls and explain which colour relates to 'At the moment I'm feeling ...' and which refers to 'Generally I am ...' Ask students to walk around the room, choosing at least one word of either colour to use in answer to the two questions on the board. Offer yourself and the dictionaries as resources if new words are encountered; students may also consult each other. When a word is chosen by two people, they should

negotiate who should get the word, or share. Ask students to sit down once they have chosen. They should 'wear' their words.

4 Organize cross-class open pair feedback, encouraging students to use the questions on the board. Students who are asking questions should find out why the answerer chose those words.

5 Divide the class into pairs or small groups and share out the remaining words on the walls between them. They should look for pairs of words with opposite meanings, visiting other groups if necessary for exchanges.

6 Groups should present their antonyms on the board. Invite peer correction. Provide the worksheet for students to check their answers against and mark the stress over each word. If mispronunciation occurs, ask for peer correction before you step in.

Follow up

Vocabulary from this activity can be recycled in a future lesson by asking students to choose from the worksheet those words which reflect qualities needed to do different jobs.

Words to describe ourselves

A **At the moment I'm feeling ...**	B **Generally I am ...**
tired/**energetic**	**HARDWORKING**/*lazy*
excited/bored	light-hearted/**serious**
tense/relaxed	*patient/impatient*
anxious/*calm*	shy/**extrovert**
enthusiastic/unenthusiastic	**competitive**/uncompetitive
inspired/uninspired	*a dreamer*/**practical**
cheerful/**sombre**	ambitious/unambitious
HOT/cold	*talkative*/quiet
alert/*unresponsive*	*highly strung*/**calm**
enthusiastic/unenthusiastic	

Where is the stress on each word?

1.3 Graph skills analysis

Teaching notes

To practise Describing English language ability and discussing it with class members.

Level Lower-intermediate and above.

One-to-one Yes, this can be used. You could fill in a graph about your ability in a language other than English for comparison, if you wish.

Class size Any.

Pre-experience learners No special requirements.

Timing 35–45 minutes depending on level.

You will need One copy of the worksheet **Our English now** (p15) per student and one for yourself, enlarged if possible or copied onto an OHT.

Potentially difficult vocabulary *bar chart, horizontal axis, vertical axis*

Procedure

1 Explain that students are going to analyze their abilities and discuss their needs in English. Put the class into small groups, or pairs, if you have a small class. First they should work out what they want to be able to do, ideally, in English; what their personal objectives are. If you wish, put this phrase on the board: 'We want to be able to ...' As the groups have to devise a statement together, this will involve quite a lot of negotiation. Go around the class, giving help where needed. If necessary, provide an example. If you speak a foreign language, you could give your own objectives; for example, if you are learning Italian, you could say, 'I want to be able to manage in any practical situation when I go on holiday to Italy'. Observe how well students work together here and during stage four also.

2 Ask a representative from each group or pair to read out their statement and encourage questions and comments from the other groups.

3 Now show the students the worksheet **Our English now** and explain that the top of the vertical axis represents them achieving the objectives they have just described. Students should fill in the sheet for themselves, individually at first. If they feel that they are

confident in a particular skill, they should draw a bar up to a high level. If, on the other hand, they feel they need a lot more practice of a particular skill to reach the desired level, the bar should be drawn lower down. Give your students one worksheet each. Give a time limit for this activity.

4 When students have finished, ask them to work in their original group (or pair) and discuss their graphs. A representative should note areas they have in common. Meanwhile, make a simple three-column table on the board. Head columns two and three: 'We are quite happy with our/We need more practice of'. Below, in column one, vertically list the skills areas (reading, speaking, etc.) mentioned on the horizontal axis of the graph.

5 When groups have finished discussing, ask for feedback from the representatives. As they give it, put a tick or asterisk next to the relevant skill on the board or OHT. Do the same for the other groups or pairs, so that by the end you can see clearly which areas most students are happy with or need to work on. It can be useful to put this information on a poster for the classroom, so that it can be periodically reviewed if possible.

Feedback

Tell students how you intend to incorporate the data from the discussion into their lessons. (How far you can do this will depend very much on the freedom you have to determine the syllabus and lesson content, but even working to a fairly strict syllabus, or prescribed textbook, you can shift the skills emphasis.)

Worksheet Graph skills analysis

Our English now

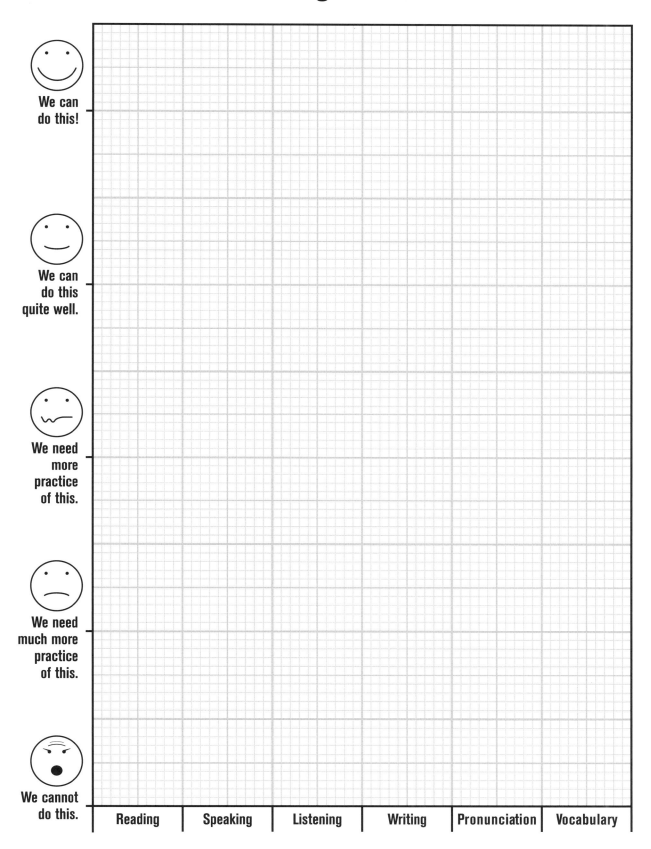

1.4 Personality scales

Teaching notes

To practise Using personality adjectives and second conditional questions to find out about someone.

Level Mid-intermediate and above.

Pre-experience learners No special requirements.

Class size Two or more.

One-to-one Yes; good for students and teacher to get to know one another better.

Overall timing Approximately 50–55 minutes. If time is short, or you wish to use this as a warmer, split **Sheet two** (p18) into two, so that each student only asks half the questions.

Potentially difficult words *flexible, intuitive, secretive, impulsive, imaginative*

You will need Two copies of **Sheet one** (p17) per student and enough copies of **Sheet two** for half your class, plus two copies of **Sheets one** and **two** for your demonstration.

NOTE: Do emphasize the light-hearted nature of this activity; it is for language practice, not psychoanalysis!

Procedure

1 Pre-teach or check students' understanding of the adjectives on **Sheet one**. You could provide one of the columns of words and ask students to find their antonyms. At higher levels, students could also find synonyms. Check the antonyms against the ones used on the sheet, but remember that there may be other possibilities.

2 Give each student a copy of **Sheet one** and ask them to write their name at the top. Explain that each line between a pair of opposing adjectives is a scale and that the students are going to mark a cross on each line to show what sort of person they are. Demonstrate this by holding up a copy. For example, if you consider yourself to be on the egocentric side for number one, mark a cross towards that end of the scale. Now ask students to fill in their own scales individually, marking all 12 scales. Students should not show each other their sheets. Provide help where necessary.

3 Ask students to hand in their completed sheets to you, to be returned later.

4 Pair students. Give out a new **Sheet one** to each student and a copy of **Sheet two** to each pair. Demonstrate, using a volunteer as a partner. Explain that the questions on **Sheet two** relate to the scales on **Sheet one**: question one is for scale one, etc. Then ask the volunteer question one, and, according to her/his answer, mark a cross on the first line on **Sheet one**. Ask the volunteer to do the same for your answer. For example, someone who said that s/he would definitely leave the piece of cake would be marked near the selfless end of the scale.

5 Ask your students to fill in all 12 scales according to their partner's answers. Make sure that the quiz is done by both students, so both have a marked chart at the end. Stress that students should not show their sheets to their partners.

6 When your students have finished, return the original sheets and ask pairs to compare the version they have just completed for their partner and their partner's original, and discuss any big differences.

Feedback

Elicit, or put on the board, some qualifying adverbs such as 'a bit', 'quite', 'very' and 'extremely'. Ask students to choose one or two of the adjectives which describe their partner, using the appropriate adverb. Give an example, such as 'Person X is very open because s/he said that s/he would enjoy hearing about a new person and would tell that person all about her/himself.' If you wish to provide a writing activity at this stage, you could ask students to write three sentences using this formula, not mentioning their partner's name. Then take in the writing, mix it up and redistribute it. Students go around the class, trying to find the author of their piece by asking questions.

Variation: With higher level groups, allow students to write their own interview questions to discover what their partner is like. **Sheet two** is not needed in this case but more support will be necessary during the activity.

Sheet one

What sort of person are you?

1 egocentric ←————————————————————→ selfless

2 competitive ←————————————————→ uncompetitive

3 solitary ←————————————————————→ sociable

4 flexible ←————————————————————→ stubborn

5 rational ←————————————————————→ intuitive

6 open ←————————————————————→ secretive

7 aggressive ←————————————————————→ gentle

8 impulsive ←————————————————————→ cautious

9 ambitious ←————————————————→ unambitious

10 careful ←————————————————————→ careless

11 well-organized ←————————————————→ disorganized

12 imaginative ←————————————————→ unimaginative

Sheet two

Questions to ask

1 Would you take the last piece of cake at a reception, if you were hungry?

2 How would you feel if a colleague of yours got the job you really wanted?

3 If you went to a party where you knew almost no one, how would you feel?

4 How would you react if a colleague disagreed with your way of approaching a work problem?

5 If you were given a new project to attempt, how would you start work on it – by analysis first or by following your instinct?

6 If a new friend whom you didn't know well told you everything about her/himself, what would you do and how would you feel?

7 If a colleague at work got angry with you about something you had done, how would you feel?

8 If you found a fantastic jacket in a shop which fitted you well and really suited you, but which you could not afford, would you still buy it?

9 How happy would you be if you did not obtain a better paid, higher level job within the next five years?

10 Would it be unusual if you lost your house or office keys?

11 If you received a lot of handouts at a conference or training day, some of which were more relevant to you than others, what would you do with them when you got back to your office?

12 Do you think that you could be successful as a writer, interior designer or TV producer? Why?/Why not?

1.5 Identity swap

Teaching notes

To practise Asking questions to obtain information about someone you do not know and summarizing the information received.

Level Lower-intermediate and above. (You will need to spend longer on stage two below if you have lower-intermediate students.)

Pre-experience learners No special preparation.

Class size Four plus, but works especially well with larger classes.

One-to-one Not suitable.

Timing 30–40 minutes.

You will need Name cards which can stand up on the desk for each student. Make these from fairly stiff card, folded over horizontally.

Procedure

This is an activity to be used in one of the first lessons with your class. It is designed so that students can find out something about each other and get used to integrating and working cooperatively. Use the activity after students have heard each other's names and have had a chance to familiarize themselves with those names.

1 Give each student their name card early on in the lesson and ask them to keep it on their table, in front of them.

2 Now elicit some questions which students could ask someone whom they do not know. Write the questions on the board and invite peer correction if there are any errors. Questions might include 'What's your name?', 'Where are you from?', 'What's your job' or 'What do you do?', 'Which company do you work for?' and 'How long have you been learning English?'

3 Give students a time limit such as five minutes for a small class and ten minutes for a larger class. Instruct students to mingle and find out as much as they can about others in class, using the questions on the board and any other questions they can think of. Emphasize that they should move around and try to talk to every member of the class. Note: It is important that students

leave their desk, and that their name card is left there as they stand up to start speaking.

4 As the activity proceeds, go around the class, encouraging any non-participators to take part, noting good language and recurring errors. Take part in the activity yourself if you wish.

5 When the time limit is up, ask students to sit down in a different seat to the one they were sitting on at the beginning. They should be sitting at a desk with someone else's name on it.

6 Tell students that they are now the person on the name card and ask each one to give some information about that person, using the first person 'I'. This should be done in a relaxed way, as the learner may not remember much about a person, particularly if the class is large. Encourage other students to help out with information if necessary, which also helps to make this part of the activity more interactive.

7 Provide language feedback from your notes in stage four and if you think it is useful, recap very briefly on what has been said, emphasizing any especially interesting facts.

Follow up

You could write a list of the special features of your students and in the next lesson, see if the class can identify to whom the feature or features belong.

2.1 Introducing yourself and others

Teaching notes

To practise Formal introductions, starting conversations with people for the first time, interrupting politely, joining in an existing conversation, spelling and checking names and giving and taking down telephone numbers.

Level Lower-intermediate and above. Conversations among higher level students will often be longer and more sophisticated, but do not have to be for the activity to be successful.

Pre-experience learners This activity should be fine for such learners if they are able to use the language of introductions and simple questions. The cards create a business atmosphere.

Class size Minimum six. However, this activity works best with a larger class (maximum 22).

One-to-one This is a group activity so is not suitable for one-to-one classes, but you could use the **Role play cards** (p21–2) as the basis for mini role plays or for writing practice of taking down details (name, company and nationality).

Timing 10–30 minutes, depending on class size and level.

You will need One set of the **Role play cards**, cut up and put into numerical order.

Note: Students need to be familiar with the language of formal introductions and polite questions to do the activity. It would probably also be of value to discuss which nationalities expect to be addressed particularly formally. This activity is useful for encouraging students to speak to other students in class with whom they may not have previously spoken.

Procedure

1 Write 'Welcome to the International Car Manufacturers' Conference' on the board. Explain that each member of the class will play a different role and that the card they will be given will give instructions about someone they should find.

If you are using this as a warmer activity, you should have the title on the board before the lesson starts and hand out the Role play cards to students as they arrive. This activity is particularly useful for classes where some students tend to arrive late.

Emphasize that this is a speaking activity so students should not show their cards to each other.

2 Students go around the class introducing themselves, giving their names, countries and companies and politely asking questions to find the person they are looking for. (Note: The surname on each card is underlined.) If necessary, they should politely interrupt and join an existing conversation.

3 When they find the person they are looking for, they should introduce themselves, say why they are interested in that person and take down their name (if not already known) and telephone number.

4 When the activity seems to be reaching its natural end, round it off by checking how many of the class succeeded in finding the person they were looking for. Those who did not can then check who it was!

Role play cards

1
Ms Ayumi/Mr Akira <u>Hara</u> (Japan/Hit Sport cars)

Tel +81-3-785600

You want to talk to a Zap representative about arranging a meeting.

Name ....

Tel ....

2
Ms Jane/Mr John Brown (U.S./Zap Motors)

You would like to make contact with a Dutch representative with the surname Petersen.

Tel ....

3
Ms Juliette/Mr Jean-Louis Jerôme (France/Reno Family cars)   Tel +33-1-974881

You need to make contact with someone from Japan to discuss possible exports to that country.

Name ....

Tel ....

4
Ms Petra/Mr Peter Holmes (England/Hall Motors)
Tel +44-1582-3478

You have had many letters from the Reno representative and would like to meet face to face now and maybe arrange for her/him to visit England.

Name ....

Tel ....

5
Ms Janine/Mr Jan Petersen (Netherlands/Dutch Trucks Ltd.)

Tel +31-70-084441

You are interested in making contact with someone from the British firm, Hall Motors.

Name .... Tel ....

6
Ms Indira/Mr Ali Raza (India/Langhams Luxury Saloon) Tel +91-22-555273

You would like to make contact with a Hit Sports cars representative.

Name ....

Tel ....

7
Ms Alina/Mr Piotr <u>Kowalski</u> (Poland/Brodski transport)

Tel +48-22-794107
You would like to meet someone from a truck company because your company would like to move into truck production with a foreign company.

Name ....

Tel ....

8
Ms Mona/Mr Abdul Eslamdoust (Saudi Arabia/Tiger transport)
                                                 Tel +966-2-570198

You are interested in meeting a representative for Langhams Luxury Saloons.

Name ....

Tel ....

9
Ms Greta/Mr Carsten <u>Garbson</u> (Germany/MBW) Tel +49-89-6794040

You want to make contact with a British representative.

Name ....

Tel ....

10
Ms Anna/Mr Sven Larsson (Sweden/Viva)
Tel +46-8-9701123

You would like to make contact with a French representative.

Name ....

Tel ....

11
Ms Marie-France/Mr Paul Lefèvre (French Guiana/Eco cars)

Tel +594-846139 ext 881

You would like to make contact with a colleague from Germany.

Name ....

Tel ....

12
Ms Mary/Mr Harry Deng (Hong Kong/ Journalist with the Hong Kong News)

Tel +852-447619 ext 47
You would like to arrange interviews with the representatives called Holmes and Hara.

Name ....

Tel ....

Name ....

Tel ....

13

Ms Tarja/Mr Pekka <u>Salonen</u>
(Finland/Star cars)
Tel +358-13-523376

You want to make contact with a Viva representative.

Name ....

Tel   ....

14

Ms Jai Quing/Han Yong <u>Wong</u> (China/Lady)

Tel +86-10-893651
You want to make contact with anyone from Hong Kong.

Name ....

Tel   ....

15

Ms Anita/Mr Paul <u>Machebe</u>
(South Africa/Classic Reproductions)
Tel +27-41-742918
You want to make contact with a representative from Finland, where there is great interest in reproductions of 1950s American cars.

Name ....

Tel ....

16

Ms Karin/Mr Ken <u>Ngoya</u> (Nigeria/Car Manufacturers' Union representative)

Tel +234-62-562134

You want to talk to a Lady representative.

Name ....

Tel ....

17

Ms Dolores/Mr Samuel <u>Lopez Dos Santos</u>
(Brazil/Supreme Saloons)
Tel +55-61-243754 ext.987
You would like to make contact with someone from South Africa.

Name ....

Tel ....

18

Ms Caterina/Mr Carlos <u>Sanchez</u> (Cuba/Car Manufacturers' Union representative)
Tel +53-7-611324

You would like to meet another union representative at the conference.

Name ....

Tel ....

19

Ms Felicity/Mr Frederick <u>Brew</u>
(Australia/Photographer for That Car magazine)

Tel +61-2-978461

You would like to meet another journalist.

Name ....

Tel ....

20

Ms Natalia/Mr Aleksander <u>Malachov</u>
(Russia/Lada)   *Tel +7-095-37614*
You would like to meet a Lada representative from a different country.

Name ....

Tel ....

21

Ms Katerina/Mr Tiberiu <u>Lymski</u>
(Bulgaria/Bulgarian National Commission for Pollution Control)
Tel +359-2-753621
You would like to make contact with someone from Finland.

Name ....

Tel ....

22

Ms Irina/Mr Itzhak <u>Cohen</u>
(Israel/Automobile Safety Commission)
Tel +972-3-543197
You would like to make contact with someone from Viva.

Name ....

Tel ....

2.2 Restaurant board game

Teaching notes

To practise The language of business lunches and making polite requests, enquiries and suggestions.

Level Lower-intermediate and above.

Pre-experience learner Use the special questions in stage 1 of the Procedure. Spend as long as you need on this to ensure that your students are familiar with the notion of the business lunch and what it entails.

Class size Two or more. Four can play easily around the board.

One to one Difficult. The game centres on group discussion of each other's performance in English, but if the teacher is sensitive and discussion of all the answers is encouraged, it can be used.

Overall timing Approximately 70–95 minutes.

Potentially difficult vocabulary *vegan, vegetarian, host(ess), mild, hot* (as in peppery), *typical(ly), spill, tactful(ly), to run out of something*

You will need One copy per group of the **Student instructions**, **Discovery cards: Information sheet** (p24) and of the **Board** (p27, enlarged to A3 size if possible); photocopy and cut out one set each per group of the **Initiative**, **Discovery** and **Cooperation cards** (p25–7); provide a set of markers, and a die or hexagonal spinner. Prepare an OHT or poster if desired (see stage 1).

Procedure

1 Tell students that this is a board game which will give them practice of dealing with typical situations they may meet during business lunches. As a warm-up, put the following questions on the board, OHP or on a poster for pairs to discuss:

What is the purpose of a business lunch?

Who normally pays for the lunch?

- If your students are business people:

  How often do you have to attend business lunches in English?

  What kind of problems do you encounter?

  Do you enjoy going to business lunches? Why?/Why not?

- If your students are pre-experience learners:

  What kind of problems could people attending business lunches in English have?

  Do you think that you would enjoy going to such business lunches? Why?/Why not?

- Allow pairs to compare experiences before getting brief feedback. Focus on predicted or actual problems experienced and put them on the board.

2 Give each group a set of materials. Point out the **Student instructions**.

3 Negotiate with your students what a 'successful performance' of a card means. Formulate this simply, on the board, focusing on areas that you have been working on. A description may use phrases such as *s/he uses good vocabulary/is grammatically correct/uses suitable intonation/communicates the meaning clearly*, etc. Once you have decided this, it should be referred to by the students during the game. Note: students should not be penalized for their pronunciation of dishes with unusual names.

4 Check if students have any questions about how to play the game.

5 Once the students seem sure of what to do, let them organize their game themselves as far as possible. This is a good opportunity for you to listen to their use of English, record some of their conversations and also observe how the students function in groups.

Feedback

Focus on general use of good expressions and common errors. As this is a free practice activity you simply round off by asking the students who won in each group.

If you record or video parts of students' games, leave feedback until after you have had an opportunity to analyze the material.

Discovery cards: Information

GOŁONKO is pig's knee in jelly.

STEAK TARTARE is made of raw (uncooked) minced steak and is usually served with a raw egg, chopped raw onions and seasoning.

SNAKE is considered a delicacy in Taiwan and is very expensive.

HARIRA is a thick chicken, chickpea and vegetable soup.

LIME PICKLE is an extremely hot pickle often eaten on deep fried, plate-sized crispy crackers called poppadums.

VINEGAR FISH contains fish so is not suitable for someone who does not like fried food. It also uses chillies, spices, lemon and vinegar.

GUACAMOLE is a thick, creamy green dip made of avocado and chilli pepper. It is hot and peppery tasting.

RATATOUILLE is a French dish made of vegetables (tomatoes, peppers, aubergines and courgettes), oil and garlic.

DAK JIM is a strong flavoured dish using garlic, chilli and soy sauce.

TARTE TATIN is an apple pie with a caramel layer on top. It is served upside down and is very sweet.

CUBAN BLACK BEANS are fried with onion, garlic, chilli, a sweet pepper and various fresh herbs.

CURRIED GOAT is a speciality from Jamaica.

CABBAGE WITH COCONUT uses only vegetables, spices and oil, so is suitable for a vegan.

BLACK FOREST GATEAU is made with chocolate, black cherries and a lot of cream. It tastes delicious but would not be suitable for someone on a diet!

GAZPACHO is a tomato soup with garlic served with pieces of cucumber in it. It is unusual because it is always served cold.

CARROT TAJINE does contain a lot of carrots but also lamb and chicken, so it is not suitable for vegetarians.

VINDALOO curry is very hot and peppery.

KORMA is a mild and creamy one made with coconut.

CHICKEN KIEV is chicken cooked with garlic butter and herbs in the middle.

Student instructions

1 Each person throws the die. The person with the highest score starts.

2 Each person chooses a marker (knife, fork, spoon or cup).

3 The person starting throws the die again and moves her/his marker forward the relevant number of squares on the board.

If s/he arrives on an odd numbered square, e.g. 1, 3, 5 s/he takes an **Initiative card**.

If s/he arrives on an even numbered square, e.g. 2, 4, s/he takes a **Discovery card**. The person reads aloud the instructions on the card, then does what the instructions say.

If the group agrees that what the person says is good enough, according to the description your teacher discussed with you, the player moves forward an extra square. If not, s/he must stay on the same square.

4 The next person throws the die and the game continues until the first player reaches the finish.

NOTE: If someone lands on the same square as another person, both of them pick up a **Cooperation card** and do the role play described, together. If the role play is good enough, BOTH players can move forward TWO squares. You can check the answers to the **Discovery card** questions by using the **Information sheet**. (Keep this face down near the board until you need it.)

Discovery cards

Lime pickle is on offer in an Indian restaurant. Ask about the taste. — *Discovery*	In Libya you want to try Carrot Tajine. Check with your hosts that it is a vegetarian dish. — *Discovery*
You are vegetarian. Can you eat ratatouille? Ask your colleague. — *Discovery*	Check if a Vindaloo or Korma curry would be better for your guest who prefers mild food to hot, spicy food. — *Discovery*
You see Guacamole on the menu at a Mexican restaurant. Check with the waiter what it contains. — *Discovery*	You are a vegan. Cabbage with coconut is on a menu in southern India. Check that it is suitable for you. — *Discovery*
In Havana you have a delicious dish called Cuban black beans. Politely ask how to make it. — *Discovery*	At a special conference dinner, you are served curried goat. Ask where the dish comes from. — *Discovery*
Your guest tells you they are trying to slim. Ask the waiter if Black Forest Gateau would be suitable for your guest. — *Discovery*	If you have a sweet tooth, will you like Tarte Tatin? Ask what it is. — *Discovery*
Your Spanish host says Gazpacho is an unusual soup. Ask why politely. — *Discovery*	In Algeria, you see a chicken dish called Dak Jim. Ask politely how strong it is. — *Discovery*
You see Harira on a menu in North Africa and want to know about it before you order. Ask. — *Discovery*	You do not drink alcohol. Check if the Italian dessert Tiramisu contains any. — *Discovery*
You see what you think is snake meat on a menu in Taiwan. Check, using a question tag (e.g. Don't you?/Isn't it?). — *Discovery*	In an English restaurant you see Toad in the Hole on the menu. Ask what it is. — *Discovery*
Check that you will enjoy steak Tartare by asking the waiter what it is made of. — *Discovery*	You don't like fried food. On a menu in Malaysia you see Vinegar Fish. Check if it is fried. — *Discovery*
You see golonko on a menu in Poland. Ask a question to check what it is. — *Discovery*	You don't like garlic. Ask what Chicken Kiev contains to see if you will like it. — *Discovery*

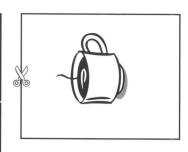

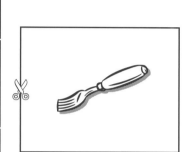

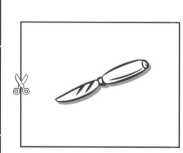

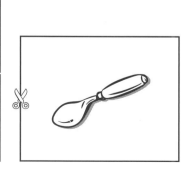

Restaurant board game markers

Initiative and Cooperation

Initiative

- You are entertaining two foreign guests in your town. You have finished eating. Offer coffee, liqueurs and any special local drink you can think of.
- You are a guest at a very formal dinner. You need to go to the toilet. What do you say?
- You accidentally spill oily salad dressing onto the tablecloth. You are the guest. What do you do or say?
- This is a non-smoking restaurant but the man at the table next to yours is smoking. Say something.
- Your colleague's meat is so overcooked that she cannot cut it. Suggest something to her.
- The waitress brings an opened bottle of wine which has 1993 on the label. You ordered an expensive 1986 bottle. What do you say?
- The waiter has brought beef soup instead of the mushroom soup you ordered. What do you say?
- A waiter gives you beer which seems to be warm. What do you say, if anything?
- You wait half an hour to be served. What do you say to your guests and to the restaurant staff?
- Your table is dirty. What do you say to the waiter?

Initiative

- You take your guest to the only good restaurant in town for lunch but it is closed. What do you say to your guest and what do you do next?
- Your colleague, who doesn't speak much English, has ordered brandy. The waiter tells you that they have run out of brandy. Explain this in simple words.
- You must leave soon to get back to the office but the waiter is very busy. Say something to get your bill.
- The menu is very long and complicated. Ask the waiter or waitress for a recommendation.
- You are at a business lunch where you must discuss a contract. The people at the next table are being very noisy. Say something.
- Your guest doesn't like the food she ordered and is not eating it. Suggest something.
- The bill arrives. It is too high. It should be £35.00 not £48.00. Complain politely.
- You booked a table for eight people and now you are at the restaurant, you realize that only seven places are set. What do you say and to whom?
- You would like a dessert. Ask the waiter or waitress for help.
- You are a guest in London. Your main course, roast beef, arrives and the meat is red. What do you say, and to whom?

Cooperation

- Your boss asked you to take a client out to lunch. You had a generous spending limit but your guest was extravagant! Role play the conversation with your boss.
- You have a vegetarian guest and the menu is full of meat! (You didn't know before the meal that the guest didn't eat meat.) Role play the conversation with the waiter or waitress.
- Your guest from Italy has eaten almost all his meal and still does not seem to want to talk business. Role play the situation, one of you playing the Italian.
- If you were entertaining a group of guests and one of them started to look very ill, what would you do? Discuss it.
- Discuss what to do when your American visitor wants to work through the lunch break and you had hoped to discuss things informally then.
- You are lunching with a Spanish client. Both of you should be back in the office already. What do you tell your guest, and your boss?
- You arrive at a restaurant with a third person who is a guest. You have 90 minutes for lunch. The table you reserved is occupied. Discuss what to do.
- You have foreign guests to lunch next week. Decide what is important about the restaurant you will choose.
- A former colleague lunches with you in your city. The bill is large. The lunch is private. Agree on how to pay it.
- Discuss how long to spend over lunch in the schedule you are preparing for a French guest next week.

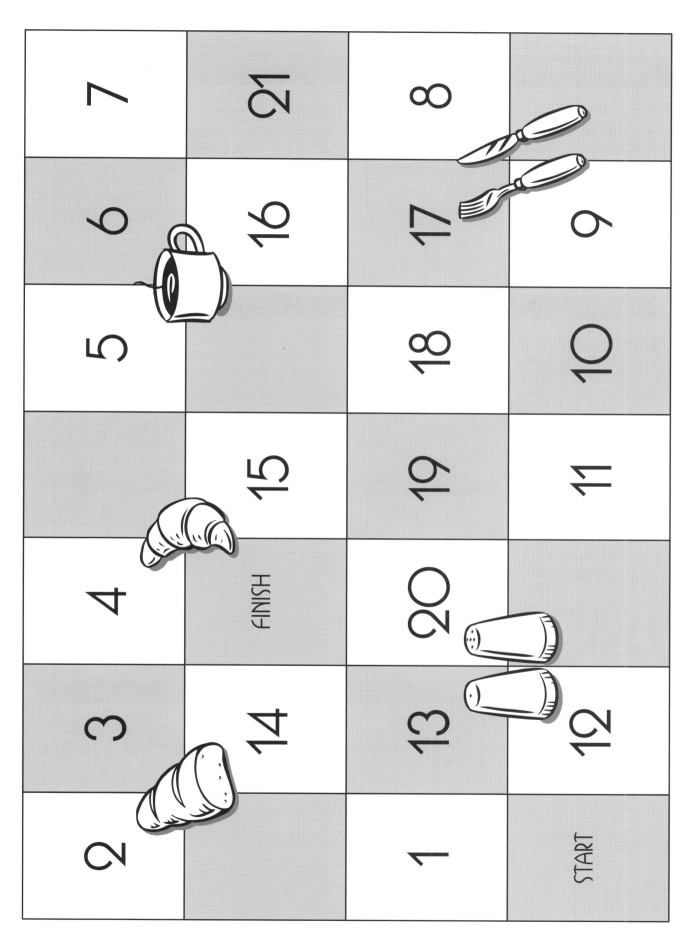

2.3 Question and answer Pelmanism

Teaching notes

To practise Recognizing and matching common questions and answers.

Level Pre-intermediate–intermediate.

Pre-experience learners No special preparation needed as this is social language.

Class size Two plus.

One-to-one You can play the game with the student, but during your turn, first ask your student to spot any pairs in your hand.

Timing 12–15 minutes,

You will need A set of **Question and answer Pelmanism cards** (p29), cut up for each group of four in your class. The question cards (printed in bold) need to be identified on the reverse side, either by mounting them on a different coloured card or by putting a large question mark on each of them.

Procedure

1 Tell students that they are going to play a card game matching typical social questions and answers in English. Demonstrate the game to them with one set of cards. Lay all the cards face down on a table.

The first person turns up three cards, at least one of which must be a question card. If any two cards match, i.e. there is an answer card that goes with a question card, s/he collects that pair and turns up two more new cards. If not, the person leaves one card turned up and turns back two. It is up to the person whether s/he leaves a question card or answer card face upwards. The next person repeats the process, except that s/he can only turn up two cards.

There are two important rules: first, there should only ever be three cards turned up at any one time; and second, the cards cannot

be all answer cards or all question cards. The winner of the game is the student who gathers as many pairs as possible.

2 Give each group a set of cards and check that they start playing the game according to the rules. You will only normally need to step in if there is a disagreement about a pair of cards. However, watch out for inaccurate pairs being collected, as this means that the remaining pairs will be disturbed. If you notice that several students have a problem with a particular question or questions, note it down.

3 If one group finishes early, get them to lay all their pairs out on the table and check that they are correct. When everyone is finished, check who the winners were. You might also like to provide feedback on any problem pairs.

Follow up

In a later lesson you could use the whole worksheet (i.e. not cut up into cards) for further practice, asking students to put together several exchanges and expand them into a dialogue, deciding on the context themselves.

Worksheet: Question and answer Pelmanism cards

Aren't you John Ahmed?	Oh, he's very reliable.	Would you like a drink?
Yes, that's right, I am.	How was your journey?	Yes please, tea.
How do you do?	A bit long, but OK.	Have you come far?
How do you do.	Haven't we met before?	Oh no, just from the hotel across the road.
Where do you come from?	I don't think we have, sorry.	May I take your coat?
From Saudi Arabia.	What have you been doing recently?	Thanks very much.
What would you like?	Oh, nothing special, the usual things.	How long are you staying?
Oh, nothing for me thanks.	How are you?	Oh, for about three days.
What's he like?	Fine, thanks.	

2.4 Asking questions

Teaching notes

To practise Forming basic questions for social situations.

Level Elementary and pre-intermediate.

Pre-experience learners No special preparation needed.

Class size Two plus.

One-to-one Yes, because the pictures provide the extra 'people'.

Overall timing 35–45 minutes.

You will need Sufficient copies of the **Photos** (pp31–2) so that each student has one photograph of a person. Copy one extra photo for you to use for demonstration purposes.

Procedure

1 Students imagine that they are at a conference. It is the coffee break on the first day and they do not know anyone. Ask how they would introduce themselves. Use mime to help with this. Write the best suggestions on the board.

2 Hold up your photograph, indicating that this is the person at the conference. Provide one question which you might ask the person, for example, 'Where are you from?'

Write this on the board and now ask elementary students to think of five more questions they could ask; pre-intermediate students should think of eight more questions. Write them down. If necessary, provide question prompts on the board to help, such as 'Do you ...?/Company?/Job?'

3 Monitor students' writing and encourage self-correction where possible. Before getting general feedback, ask students to work in pairs, comparing the questions they have written.

4 Now ask each student in turn to write one of their questions on the board. Encourage peer correction and discussion of the questions'

appropriateness. This will be particularly important with multicultural classes, and differences may arise about what are and are not acceptable questions. For example, can you or should you talk about money, age or whether someone is married or not in the first discussion? Make notes on any areas of great dispute to use in the follow-up discussion.

5 Now ask the students who have the same photo to get together and consider what the pictured person's answers to the questions might be. (In small classes students can work alone or discuss their own and their partner's photo.) They should take notes.

6 Now ask for a volunteer from each pair to come and sit in your seat, or the one at the front, holding up their photo. Students ask their questions and the person at the front pretends to be the person in the photo and responds accordingly. If this goes well and students are confident, encourage extra, spontaneous questions. Let the group discuss the photo and the answers afterwards. Repeat the process with each photograph .

Feedback

Comment on good language used and any common problems.

Follow up

If there was a dispute in stage four, organize a class discussion of what is and is not acceptable in a first, fairly formal conversation with someone in their country. Discuss how to avoid difficulties where possible. Written follow up could be in the form of the imaginary dialogue with the person in the picture.

Cambridge Business English Activities © Cambridge University Press 2000

3.1 A telephone maze

Teaching notes

To practise Telephone language and responding to a range of problems on the phone.

Level Mid-intermediate and above.

Pre-experience learners S/he will need to be introduced to standard functional language for telephoning and to practise recognizing etiquette for calling. Recorded material from the business English repertoire could be used in the process.

Class size Two plus.

One-to-one This works best if the teacher is the receiver of the calls.

Overall timing 30–35 minutes.

Before class Copy sufficient **Caller sheets** (p34) for half the class, and an equal number of **Receiver sheets** (p35) for the other half of the class. Cut out the cards on the **Caller sheets**.

Procedure

1 Elicit from the students a list of rules for making a successful phone call in English. It may include: checking details, asking the speaker to repeat where necessary and being clear. Write up the list on the black/whiteboard.

2 Split the class into two. Give one group the Caller cards and sheet and the other the Receiver sheet. Allow time for the students to read the instructions and help each other understand what they are to do. Spot check to see if the groups understand their roles. Emphasize that if the callers follow the rules on the board, they will progress quicker!

3 Assign each member of the caller's group a partner from the receiver's group. Students should keep their sheets to themselves. Ask the callers to start using the instructions on their first card (A). Receivers should start with instruction 1.

4 Listen as students carry out the role play and gently assist where necessary. Note down good and weak language for feedback later.

5 When all the pairs have finished, find out which caller completed the maze in the fewest moves.

Feedback

Provide brief oral feedback from your notes in stage four. Remember to start with praise!

Sheet 1: Caller

A telephone maze: Can you find your way out?

You are the caller: phone your partner, starting with the instructions on card A, and following on with B, C, etc. Your aim is to reach card E and arrange a meeting in as few moves as possible. Your partner receives your calls and has instructions about how to respond to you. If you are clear, polite and check everything, you will progress quickly. If not, you will be delayed, so beware!

(A) **Phone Sandra Brown. You wish to arrange a meeting with her.**

(B) **Try to contact Sandra Brown using the new number.**

(C) **Phone Sandra Brown again. Your number is 01625 328 4994.**

(D) **Sandra Brown does not phone back. Try again.**

(E) **Explain that you would like to meet her this week to discuss an important matter. A short meeting would be OK and you can make any time this week.**

Sheet 2: Receiver

A telephone maze: Can your partner find the way out?

You are the person receiving the calls. Your job is to check that the caller is as clear and polite as possible on the phone.

Every time you use one of the instructions, mark it in the box below. (You may do this more than once.) The caller's aim is to get to box 20 in the smallest number of moves. There is a chart at the bottom of the page to show you the possible moves.

1	3	5	7	9	11	13	15	17	19
2	4	6	8	10	12	14	16	18	20

1 Answer the call. If the caller gives her/his name clearly, go to **4**. If not, go to **2**.

2 Ask for the caller's name and company. If s/he speaks slowly and clearly, go to **4**. If not, go to **3**.

3 Ask the caller to repeat her/his name and company clearly. Now go to **4**.

4 Offer the caller another number where s/he might get Sandra Brown: 0155 908 5333. If the caller repeats the number to check it, go to **6**. If not, go to **5**.

5 Ask the caller to repeat the number to you, to check it. Now go to **6**.

6 Finish the call and go to **7**.

7 The caller has the wrong number. Your number is 0155 918 5333. If the caller checks her/his number, go to **9**. If not, go to **8**.

8 Ask the caller to check the number s/he requires. Now go to **9**.

9 Finish the call and go to **10**.

10 You are Sandra Brown's colleague. Explain that Sandra is not in the office. If the caller asks you to take a message, go to **13**. If not, go to **11**.

11 Ask the caller if s/he would like you to take a message for Sandra. If the caller gives the message slowly and clearly, go to **13**. If not, go to **12**.

12 Ask the caller to repeat her/his message more clearly. Now go to **13**.

13 Take the message. Thank the caller and finish the call. Now go to **14**.

14 You are Sandra Brown. Apologize that you did not phone back. You had urgent business. Say that you did not recognize the caller's name and ask to check it. If the caller spells her/his name, go to **16**. If not, go to **15**.

15 Ask the caller to spell her/his name, then go to **16**.

16 Write down the name, thank the caller and ask her/him what s/he was calling for. Now go to **17**.

17 Explain that you are going abroad in a few days and ask if the meeting can wait until the end of next week. If the caller offers an alternative meeting date, go to **20**. If the caller does not offer a date, but reacts politely, go to **19**. If the caller is impatient or rude, go to **18**.

18 Explain firmly that your trip abroad cannot be cancelled and is very important. If the caller makes an alternative suggestion for a meeting date, go to **20**. If not, go to **19**.

19 Offer an early morning meeting time this week, before you go away. Now go to **20**.

20 Agree on a date for a short meeting and then finish the call.

CONGRATULATIONS! YOU HAVE REACHED THE END OF THE MAZE.

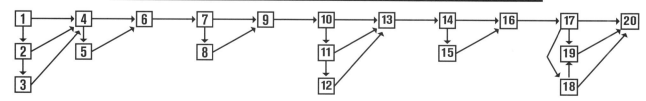

3.2 Phone quartets

Teaching notes

To practise Telephone language for a variety of purposes and recognizing good use of language in others.

Level Lower-intermediate and above. Higher level students can elaborate on and extend the role plays.

Pre-experience learners Yes, but emphasize stage one of the procedure below.

Class size Multiples of four are best, but extra students can join a quartet as an extra monitor or agree to share a particular role, e.g. they alternate B1's roles.

One-to-one This is not a suitable activity.

Overall timing 40–60 minutes.

Potentially difficult vocabulary *react, clockwork (mice), available*

You will need One copy each of **Sheets A** and **B** (p37–8) per group of four students. Cut out the **Role play cards**. Keep A and B groups separate. Optional: sticky labels in stage three; cardboard cutout telephone handsets for stage five.

Procedure

1 Preparation: With inexperienced or lower level students, ensure that they are familiar with at least the basic language to carry out the role plays. You could do this with listening, vocabulary and more controlled speaking exercises.

2 Elicit criteria for a successful phone caller and write these up on the board. You might have *is polite, clear, checks details, spells words* etc.

3 Put the class into groups of four and then split each four into two pairs. Each pair should sit side by side, opposite the other pair. Designate one pair as Pair A and the other as Pair B and ask the students to choose within each pair if they are Student number one (i.e. A1/B1) or two (A2/B2). It can help for students to wear labels saying A1, A2, B1. B2.

4 Place a pile of the appropriate **Role play cards** face down in front of each pair. Explain that they will take it in turns to perform a role play with one of the people opposite them and that the other pair will monitor and mark their colleagues' performance. The criteria on the board should be used and a familiar marking system decided on, such as A–E or 1–10.

5 A1 and B1 turn up their first **Role play cards** on their pile and then start their first call. (It can increase authenticity for students to turn away from each other slightly when they call, and also to be given a cardboard cutout of a telephone handset.) When the first call is over, the monitors (other listeners) confer and give the pair a mark, which is noted down. A2 and B2 now do their role play and the activity continues until all eight role plays have been done. Listen to your students, make notes on the language used, and offer help if you are needed.

Feedback

Ask each quartet which pair scored the highest overall and why. Provide feedback from your notes.

Sheet A: role play cards

(A1) First conversation

Give the information requested.

(A2) Second conversation

Phone B2 in the other pair and ask for his/her bank account number. (Don't forget to check and be polite!)

(A1) Third conversation

Phone B1 in the other pair and arrange a meeting:
– at your company
– on either Monday at 14.00 or Wednesday at 17.00.
Check all the details!

(A2) Fourth conversation

The order mentioned has not yet been sent. Apologize and explain that there have been production problems recently for those goods. Don't forget to write the order number down!

(A1) Fifth conversation

Direct flights to New York are available on Mondays, Thursdays and Saturdays. They all leave at 08.15. Single economy fare is $870. Business class single is $1,350. Return (economy) is $1,200. Return (business) is $2,050.

(A2) Sixth conversation

Phone B2 and explain that you cannot attend the board meeting on Friday. Explain why. (YOU think of a reason.)

(A1) Seventh conversation

Phone B1 and cancel the meeting you arranged for Monday. Explain the reason (YOU think of one!) and suggest another time.

(A2) Eighth conversation

Mr Jonkins is not available today. Take a message.

Remember to check everything.

Sheet B: role play cards

(B1) First conversation

Phone A1 and ask him/her to give you his/her address. Don't forget to be polite and check everything!

(A2) Second conversation

Phone B2 in the other pair and ask for his/her bank account number. (Don't forget to check and be polite!)

(B1) Third conversation

You are free to attend a meeting only on Wednesday after 5.30 p.m. (It's a very busy week.)

(B2) Fourth conversation

Phone A2 and ask if the order for goods Ref: AXJ 429/Z has been dealt with yet.

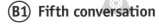

(B1) Fifth conversation

Phone A1 and ask about flights to New York City from your city. Ask about days, times and prices. Write down all the details and check that you have got them right.

(B2) Sixth conversation

React to the caller's comments appropriately.

(B1) Seventh conversation

You cannot attend any meetings next week because you will be in St. Petersburg. The week after next you are quite free. React suitably to the caller's comments.

(B2) Eighth conversation

Phone A2 and give Mr Jonkins in the Sales Department this information:
– The clockwork mice have arrived and will be stored in Montreal.
– They cost $1.50 each.

3.3 What not to do

Teaching notes

To practise Telephoning and negotiating language, being tactful and dealing with impolite behaviour on the phone.

Level Intermediate and above.

Pre-experience learners This activity can be used when students have become familiar with the conventions of business calls.

Class size Two or more, although a better atmosphere is usually achieved with slightly larger classes. With a maximum of seven, each student gets the chance to be both a caller and receiver; with 14, students have the chance to play just one of these roles.

One-to-one This can be done if you swap caller and receiver roles and maybe record the lesson to discuss intonation afterwards.

Overall timing If all the cards are used, a minimum of 20 minutes; with students who develop the role plays further, up to 40 minutes.

You will need One copy of the **Role play cards** (p40), cut out.

Procedure

1 If you have experienced business people in your class, you could ask them to tell the class about the most difficult person they ever had on the phone. Find out who had the worst! If you have pre-experience learners, get them to imagine a difficult person answering the phone; what would they do or say? Makes notes on the board as your students describe the people. Words like *impolite*, *impatient* and *intolerant* may appear.

2 Explain that students are going to practise being and dealing with difficult people on the phone; people who have the qualities given on the board. Demonstrate the first role play, being the grumpy, impatient receiver of a call, with the student who has the role play card requiring her/him to be as polite as possible.

3 Now continue, giving out one card at a time. If the class has seven or fewer students in it, allow each student to make a call and receive one. Encourage those students who are observing the role plays to comment on what happens and discuss what they would do in such a situation.

4 You decide when to call a halt. Using all the cards is unnecessary, especially with a small class.

Feedback

Provide feedback, focusing on tone of voice and expressions for being tactful, for example, 'I understand that you are feeling angry about this, but I am afraid that I cannot change the situation', or 'Perhaps we can come to some sort of compromise?'

Role play cards

(1) You need a day off next month to take your English language exams. Phone and politely ask your boss if this is possible.

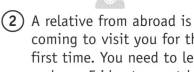

(2) A relative from abroad is coming to visit you for the first time. You need to leave early on Friday to meet her at the airport. Phone and ask your boss.

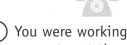

(3) You were working on your computer at the office when suddenly all the material has disappeared from the screen. Phone technical support and ask for advice and help.

(4) You are a new security guard. You notice that one of the senior managers always parks their car by the front door, making it difficult for people to get in and out. Phone and politely suggest that they use the staff car park nearby.

(5) You are a secretary. Phone the catering manager to ask if it is possible to offer some healthier options in the staff canteen.

(6) You have received an invoice from a consulting company which seems to be far too high. (It is £600 and you expected it to be £350.) Phone the company to check this and ask for a replacement to be sent urgently.

(7) You have to go abroad on urgent business. You will be back late on Friday evening. Phone your colleague to explain that you cannot make the meeting you arranged for Friday. Suggest a Saturday meeting instead.

4.1 Formal or informal?

Teaching notes

To practise Recognizing formal and less formal register in letters, and organizing a letter logically.

Level Intermediate and upper-intermediate. Possibly omit stage one below with an experienced class and see **below for higher levels.

Class size One plus.

One-to-one A good activity for one-to-one that allows the student to take the initiative.

Overall timing About 30 minutes.

Potentially difficult vocabulary *wig, a bulk supply, retail, expand* (a range), *to be snowed under* (by paperwork), *a get-together*

You will need One copy of the three **Letters** (pp42–4) for every three students in your group, cut into strips, mixed up together and kept as a set. Optional: copies of the letters not cut up, sufficient for each student, or photocopy the letters onto OHTs.

Procedure

1 Revise the basic phrases of formal, semi-formal and informal letters. You could do this by drawing three large rectangles on the board and getting volunteers to add the skeleton phrases of letters in the correct places. Check with context questions when a letter will be very formal or less formal. For example: 'If you write "Dear Ms Cordell" at the beginning of a letter, how well do you know me?' Answer: I have a fairly formal relationship with you; you are not a friend, or someone I know well. (Note that in some cultures, a more formal manner of address is used even when you know someone well.)

2 Put students into groups of three and give them the strips. Indicate with one set of strips that three different letters have become mixed up; ask students first to separate the sentences into three piles, according to letters. They could take one letter each. **A brief description of the letters is given on their instruction slip, but this is optional for higher levels, as the activity is more challenging without it. Check any recurring problems for feedback later.

3 When most groups have got the strips into three reasonably accurate piles, ask them to try to put each letter in the correct order. (Quick groups may have started to do this automatically.) At this stage, students often correct their own work from stage two. If one group finishes early, you could ask them to consider how the sentences in each letter may be divided into paragraphs.

4 For feedback, ask a student to read his/her letter aloud and allow peer correction. Ask different students to read out the second and third letters. Note that particularly for the third letter, students may well find acceptable alternatives to the original.

5 Provide copies of the three letters if you wish, as some students like having a model to check.

Follow up

Students write a reply to one of the letters. You could then get students to correct each other's letters in the following lesson.

Instructions

There are three letters here. One is a letter of application for a job, the second is a business letter written to a colleague whom the writer knows quite well and the third is a letter to a friend. Which letter would you expect to be most and least formal?

**23 Cherry Tree Walk
Appleden
Dorset
DS6 7PR**

Z.F.G Recruitment Agency
Block 5
Burnton Business Park
Dorset
DS12 9LK

12 February 2000

Dear Sir or Madam

I am writing in reponse to your advertisement in the *Evening Herald* yesterday for a legal secretary.

I enclose a copy of my CV as requested and would also like to briefly explain why I think that I am suitable for the job.

I recently obtained a diploma from the Association of Legal Secretaries, with distinction.

Prior to this, I worked for several solicitors as a general administrative assistant.

I am hardworking, well-organized and have a good telephone manner.

I feel that I fulfil the criteria which you describe in your advertisement and would ask you to consider me for the post.

I look forward to hearing from you.

Yours faithfully

Miss Jean A Dobson

LINDEN AND LINDEN LTD
HAIR PRODUCTS INTERNATIONAL
192 Worth Ave
Bucks
BH3 4OT

Mr Harold Green
Theatre Suppliers
56 Walden Lane
Ludlow
SJ4 5HU

12 February 2000

Dear Mr Green

Thank you for sending me the information which I asked you for concerning your company's new wig range.

We are pleased that you have been able to expand the range considerably since last year and feel sure that we will wish to order a bulk supply from you shortly.

However, you omitted to supply a price list with the new catalogue and this makes it very difficult for us to do our costings.

Are your products remaining at last year's prices, or is that over optimistic of us to assume?(!)

I would be grateful if you could send on the new price list as soon as possible as we will need to order our retail stock within the next three weeks.

I look forward to receiving the list soon. Meanwhile, I hope that the business is going well.

Please pass on my best regards to your colleague, John Harvard, whom I had the pleasure of meeting at the recent trade fair.

Yours sincerely

Jerome K Linden

Co-Director
Linden and Linden Ltd

Bickerton's Pickles
16 Palace Crescent
Bromley
BR2 HT7

Friday, 5th September 2000

Dear Sally

It was great to see you again at the conference last week and catch up a bit.

It was a good event, don't you think?

I managed not to fall asleep in any of the presentations!

(Only joking of course!)

I thought your workshop was particularly good by the way.

I am glad that your new job is going well but worry that you are getting a bit snowed under with paperwork.

(I suppose that that is a danger for all of us at times though!)

We all miss you here at Bickerton's.

So how about coming over here for lunch one Friday and having a get-together with all your old pals from the company?

How about Friday 28th?

Let me know whether you can make it and I'll book a table.

If not, don't worry. Send me some other dates you could do.

Look forward to hearing from you soon then.

Best wishes

Nina

4.2 Writing a CV

Teaching notes

To practise Asking past tense questions, talking about past experience, obtaining basic information about someone, using time prepositions and spelling.

Level Lower-intermediate and above.

Pre-experience learner Where students have not yet gained any work experience this will make the activity a little shorter, as that section of the CV cannot be filled. If they wish, students can imagine a job they would like to do, or would like to have done.

Class size An even number is best; if you have an odd number, make one group of three.

One-to-one This is a good activity to do with your student as it helps you to get to know each other better. If, however, you or the student do not wish to divulge your secrets, you could use imaginary lives or the lives of famous people. This also applies to groups who do not wish to provide details of themselves.

Overall timing 35–60 minutes depending on level.

You will need One copy of the blank CV (p46) per student.

Procedure

1 In pairs or small groups, students discuss what they think a CV (American English, résumé) is, what it's for and who you might send it to, what you should include on it, what order it should be in and how it should be laid out. Put their ideas on the board then discuss the issues together. There may be a variety of ideas on what a CV should look like and consist of. Encourage discussion of how CVs differ from country to country, and how students would compile a CV if they were applying for a job in an English-speaking country. Aim to have a list of key points for this CV presented in the correct order.

2 Explain that students are going to work with a partner to fill in a CV for them. Using the list of points on the board, elicit suitable questions that could be asked to obtain the information. You could ask a student to write the questions on the board next to each CV point and encourage their peers to correct. Example questions would be, 'Which school did you go to?' 'What was your first job?'

3 Provide each student with a CV sheet and divide the class into pairs. It is important to emphasize that the student must fill in the sheet for their partner, not for themselves. Monitor the activity, checking language used and making your own notes. Encourage students to spell out unusual words rather than resorting to writing them down to copy. Also make sure that they check that what they have written is correct.

4 Round off the activity either by asking each student to give you the most interesting fact they have discovered about their partner, or by reorganizing the pairs and asking students to tell the new partner about the old partner's CV.

5 Provide feedback on the notes you made while you were monitoring the activity. You could also discuss how the CV students have been filling in differs from the one they are used to in their culture; for example, age and marital status are important in some cultures.

CV

Curriculum Vitae

SURNAME

FIRST NAME(S)

ADDRESS

TELEPHONE (Work)

(Home)   Fax

Email

EDUCATION

Dates	Institution	Qualifications

WORK EXPERIENCE

Dates	Company/Organization	Job titles/duties

OTHER RELEVANT INFORMATION/SKILLS

HOBBIES AND INTERESTS

REFERENCES

4.3 A letter to correct

Teaching notes

To practise Recognizing errors in a business letter. Correcting errors and editing written work.

Level Intermediate and upper-intermediate.

Pre-experience learners Students will need to be familiar with the format of business letters and standard phrases from them before doing this activity.

Class size Any.

One-to-one Yes, but it may be better for the student to correct the letter during self-study so that discussion of their answers takes place during the lesson.

Overall timing 30–45 minutes.

You will need One copy of the **Worksheet** (p48) per student, plus OHTs and OHT pens or a large sheet of paper (A1 size if possible) and marker pens. One copy of the **Model letter** per student.

Procedure

1 Explain that a Polish businesswoman, Mrs Sztuk, had to write a letter in English to a British businesswoman who will be visiting her company. Unfortunately she did not have much time to do it and has not practised her English for some time. Therefore, she has asked you to check it before she sends it.

2 Hand out one copy of the **Worksheet** to each pair of students. Encourage them to work on the corrections together. Tell students that they must check the letter for errors of grammar, spelling and punctuation and underline them on the copy. Go around the class and help out where necessary.

3 Next, provide each pair with a blank OHT with an OHT pen, or large sheet of paper and

markers. They should write their own improved version of the letter. This imitates the process students should go through when producing a high quality piece of written work.

4 When students have completed their versions display each one in turn, either on the OHP or on the wall as appropriate. Praise good use of English in each one, and invite the whole class to suggest improvements where necessary. Encourage discussion of why changes had to be made to the original letter.

5 After students' work has been analyzed, hand out the **Model letter** for their reference.

Follow up

Students could write a short reply to Mrs Sztuk's letter.

Worksheet

Ms J Lewis
Slimtone plc,
13 Broad Walk
Birmingham
BR5 6BY
UK

2-28-1999,

Chemikraz Ltd
ul. Krakowa 48
60700 Poznan
Poland

Dear Ms Jean Lewis!

I am writting thanking you for your letter which has arrived recently. I am such pleased that you can visiting us next month. We looking forward to the welcome of you!

In here are some informations about our country and yours accomadations.

Despite it is spring, almost, weather here is being still quiet cold so please bring the warm cloths with you. I will defintly recomend a hat also and hevy coat too.

When you visit our company, please to call at reception firstly, asking for myself. Then you would be take up to my office.

You will be stay at local hotel named Hotel Orit. Adres of hotel is Zwycestwa street number 56 and number of telephone is +48-61-95483. Hotel Orit is small but frendly with restaurant and room servis. You will eat there your brekfasts but I will invite you for lunchis and dinners in others places.

If you are having any questions, please inform immediately. For contact: +48-61-46289 extention 209.

With all good greetings.

Yours sincerly,

Manager of Human Resources.
Mrs. P. Sztuk

Model letter

Corrected words and phrases are in bold, but please note that this is only one possible correct version of the letter. There are many others which are accurate and valid.

Ms J Lewis
Slimtone PLC
13 Broad Walk
Birmingham
BR5 6BY
UK

28 February 1999

Chemikraz Ltd
ul. Krakowa 48
60700 Poznan
Poland

Dear Ms Lewis

I am **writing to thank** you for your letter which **arrived** recently. I am **so** pleased that you can **visit** us next month. We are looking forward to **welcoming** you.

Here **is** some **information** about our country and **your accommodation**.

Despite it **being almost** spring, **the** weather here is still **quite** cold so please bring warm **clothes** with you. I **would definitely recommend** a hat and a **heavy** coat too.

When you visit our company, please call at reception **first and ask** for **me**. Then you **will be taken** up to my office.

You will be **staying** at **a** local hotel **called** the **Orit Hotel. The address** of **the** hotel is **56** Zwycestwa **Street** and **the telephone** number is +48-61-95483. Hotel Orit is small but **friendly** with **a** restaurant and room **service**. You will eat your **breakfast there** but I will invite you for **lunch** and **dinner** in **other** places.

If you **have** any questions, please **contact me** immediately. **My telephone number is:** +48-61-46289 **extension** 209.

Yours **sincerely**

Mrs P Sztuk

Human Resources Manager

4.4 A group letter

Teaching notes

To practise Organizing a simple business letter using conjunctions and working cooperatively.

Level Lower to intermediate. (Can be used as a warmer activity at higher levels.)

Pre-experience learners Use the activity in the context of writing business letters after students are fairly familiar with their format.

Class size Ideally, 7–16 students. It can be done with smaller groups but is less challenging if it is.

One-to-one You can ask your student to: a) Put the strips in order, or b) keep the second half of each sentence yourself and ask the student to predict what follows each of her/his strips before providing the appropriate one.

Overall timing About 12 minutes. With the extension activity, 22 minutes.

You will need One cut-up letter: **strip version** (p51) for the whole class, plus one letter: **original version** (p52) per student.

Procedure

1 Distribute the strips among your students so that each has one or two. They should not read other students' strips.

2 Explain that all the strips together make a business letter replying to an application for a job. Students may only put the letter together by reading aloud and listening. You are not going to help them. They should organize themselves.

3 Sit back, slightly away from the students, as they work out the activity. Resist the temptation to 'help'.

4 When students are happy that they have worked out the letter, provide them with copies of the original letter.

Feedback

Ask the group to tell you about any differences they noticed between their version of the letter and the original one.

Extension activity

At the end of stage three above, ask students to dictate the letter to each other, each student reading out their strip(s). This is good practice for speaking clearly, listening for detail, checking and spelling. Once they have finished, give students a copy of the original letter to check against their version.

Follow up

You could ask your students to write a reply to the letter saying whether or not they can come to the interview.

Letter: strip version

Elia Haircare Products PLC, 23 Kensington Way, London, NW3 8UH

Dear Mrs Jones

Thank you for your letter applying for a post in our sales department,

which we received yesterday.

We are very interested in your application

and would like to interview you.

The interview we have arranged for you

is on Thursday 14 December at 2 pm.

The interview will take place in room 62,

which is opposite the reception desk.

Please could you confirm

that you will be able to attend.

We look forward

to hearing from you soon.

Yours sincerely

Ms Joan Armatring

Personnel manager

Letter: original version

Elia Haircare Products PLC
23 Kensington Way
London
NW3 8UH

4 December 1999

Mrs R Jones
67 Marle Avenue
London
W8 3NM

Dear Mrs Jones

Thank you for your letter applying for a post in our sales department, which we received yesterday. We are very interested in your application and would like to interview you.

The interview we have arranged for you is on Thursday 14 December at 2 pm.

The interview will take place in room 62 which is opposite the reception desk.

Please could you confirm that you will be able to attend.

We look forward to hearing from you soon.

Yours sincerely

Ms Joan Armatring

Personnel manager

4.5 Keeping it brief

Teaching notes

To practise Writing a memo or fax after skimming and scanning a text.

Level Elementary or intermediate/upper-intermediate.

Pre-experience learners No special preparation needed.

Class size Two plus.

One-to-one Yes.

Overall timing Elementary: 75–90 minutes. Intermediate/upper-intermediate: 45–75 minutes.

Potentially difficult vocabulary Elementary: *squid, prawns, trout, cod, pastry*

You will need One copy of the appropriate level **Questions** (p54–5) and a **Worksheet** (p56–7) per student. The two sets of questions for that level on either separate OHTs or different sheets of a flipchart/poster. A newspaper or company report and a local transport timetable. Blank OHTs and non-permanent pens.

Procedure

1 Introduce the topic of skim reading by opening the newspaper/report and flipping the pages. Ask if students sometimes do the same thing when they read a paper, to get a general idea of its contents. Give them a brief run down of the impression you receive by skimming. Now use the timetable to explain what scan reading is. Ask if students would ever read the whole thing in detail, and why not. Elicit the idea of scan reading for a select piece of information.

2 Provide each student with a **Questions** sheet and a **Worksheet**, face down so they cannot see it. Write the first question (from A) on the board (or reveal it if you are using an OHT). Now give your students 30 seconds to check the answer by turning over their sheets and skimming the information there.

Answers
Elementary: 1) No (3 courses).

Intermediate/Upper-intermediate: 1) Yes (good choice of meals, sports, dance and theatre).

3 Now reveal all the **part A** questions and provide a time limit for students to answer the 'scan' questions (about three to five minutes).

Answers
Elementary: 2) Soup, melon, garlic mushrooms, vegetarian *vol-au-vent* and all desserts. 3) Fisherman's pie or trout. 4) Cheese and biscuits/fruit salad without ice cream. 5) Squid, *vol-au-vent*, trout or spaghetti.

Intermediate/Upper-intermediate: 2) No, VAT is excluded. 3) Single rooms, the crèche, audio-visual equipment and the conference banquet. 4) 10 basic rooms = £600 for one night. 5) £10. 6) £20. 7) 45 minutes (7.15–8.00 am).

4 When the time is up, students compare their answers in pairs, then give you feedback.

5 Tell students they now have to write an urgent memo (for elementary level) or fax (for intermediate/upper-intermediate level). It will be based on the text they have been scanning. Display **Questions part B**. Emphasize the time limit (30 minutes, elementary; 20, intermediate/upper-intermediate). This will encourage students to scan and skim read. Students should work in pairs or threes, with one person as secretary. If possible, give students an OHT and pens so their work can be discussed with the class as soon as they have finished.

Feedback

With texts written on OHT, display to the class, praise good language and invite peer/self-correction of errors. If the texts are on paper, take them in, mark and provide group feedback next session (see section on this).

Questions: Elementary

Part A

1 Are four courses offered on this menu?

2 If you do not eat meat or fish, what can you eat at this restaurant?

3 What would you ask for if you liked fish?

4 Which is the best dessert if you do not like sweet food?

5 If you like salad with your main course, what should you order?

Part B

Writing a memo

Your manager is going to have some visitors next week and wants to take them out for an informal lunch locally.

She has asked you to find out what *The Jolly Robin* offers and send her a memo today. The memo should be as brief as possible and answer the manager's questions:

1 The company wants to pay a maximum of £17.00 per person. How much would an average three course lunch with drinks be at *The Jolly Robin*?

2 Is there a reasonable choice of dishes, including at least one vegetarian option?

3 Can we book for a party of 15 people the day before? (The visitors' schedule has to be flexible.)

Note: You have an important meeting in half an hour, so you must write this memo before then.

So for starters, that's four melons, one without the cherry, one with a strawberry instead of a cherry …

Questions: Intermediate/upper-intermediate

Part A

1 Does the venue seem to offer a good range of catering and leisure facilities?

2 Are all prices inclusive?

3 Which facilities do you have to book in advance?

4 What's the cheapest way to accommodate a group of 40 people together for one night?

5 What's the price difference between the cheapest twin room and the most expensive single room?

6 If you ordered three meals a day plus morning coffee and full afternoon tea, how much would be the catering cost per person, per day?

7 If a train arrived at Wigglington station at 7.15 am, how long would participants have to wait for the first special conference coach?

Part B

Writing a fax

A small group of Scandinavian employees from your Swedish and Danish subsidiaries are coming to visit next week and wish to hold a three-day conference to present ideas and information to managers from your head office. They have heard that Wigglington Hall may be suitable and have asked you to check. The leaflet from the Hall has been on your desk for over a week and now your secretary has left you this urgent message.

URGENT!   10.15 am

Mr Kastrup from the Danish subsidiary called.
Please send him a fax today by 12 noon.
(Fax no: +45-12-348790.) He needs to know about these things:

● Facilities for children and families

● Single room options

● Flexible catering or fixed meals included in price of room? (Prefers flexibility.)

● Small meeting rooms for up to 28 people (must have audio-visual equipment and word processors).

It is now 11.30 am. You have about 20 minutes to write the fax, allowing ten minutes to send it. (The machine is sometimes busy.) Scan the leaflet for the information you want to include and write the fax.

Menu

The Jolly Robin

Starters

Melon boat – half a melon with cherry and a slice of orange	£1.75
Cream of mushroom soup	£1.50
Prawn cocktail – seafood favourite with tangy mayonnaise	£2.35
Pâté and toast – made with lamb's liver	£2.00
Garlic mushrooms – gently cooked in butter, garlic and herbs	£1.90

Main Courses

Deep fried squid with chips and salad	£7.80
Steak au poivre with baked potato and two vegetables	£8.95
Shepherd's pie – minced beef, onion and tomatoes topped with crispy mashed potato; served with two vegetables	£5.95
Fisherman's pie – cod in a creamy sauce with mashed potato and cheese topping	£5.95
Vegetarian vol-au-vent – a mixture of fresh vegetables in a light, puff pastry case served with a large salad	£5.95
Trout with almonds accompanied by bread and butter and a green salad	£7.95
Spaghetti supreme – beef in a tomato, mushroom and onion sauce on a bed of fresh pasta; served with salad	£6.45

Desserts

Double chocolate gâteau served with fresh cream	£2.50
Fresh fruit salad (plus ice cream, 50p extra)	£2.35
English trifle (sponge cake with sherry, fruit, custard and cream)	£3.00
Fruit sorbet – a frozen dessert made with fruit, sugar and water	£2.50
A selection of cheese and biscuits	£3.00

Drinks

Wines ranging from £7.00 per bottle for house red or white to £20 for champagne. See wine list.	
Fruit juices, minerals and sparkling water	90p
Coffee	£1.10
Tea	£1.00
Herbal teas	£1.10
A full range of liqueurs available from £2.20–£3.50 each	

PARTY BOOKINGS WELCOMED. (Please book at least 24 hours in advance)

Worksheet: Intermediate/upper-intermediate

WIGGLINGTON HALL

CONFERENCE FACILITIES

Accommodation

Lecture hall (*seats 300*)	£500 per day
Minor hall (*seats 50*)	£100 per day
Lecture rooms (*15 available, seat 25 people*)	£25 per day
20 twin standard* rooms for two people	£40 one night
Four single standard* rooms	£35 one night
Five luxury twin rooms with ensuite bathroom	£60 one night
Two luxury single rooms with ensuite bathroom	£50 one night
15 basic rooms for four people sharing with washing facilities outside the room	£60 one night
Five family rooms (*double bed plus bunk beds*)	£65 one night

Standard rooms have their own washbasin but no shower or bath.

Single room provision is limited; please book well in advance.

PLEASE NOTE THAT PRICES ARE PER ROOM, NOT PER PERSON.

Leisure

Dance hall with disco facilities	£300 per day
Theatre (seats 350)	£600 per day
Gymnasium (price includes staffing)	£400 per day
Use of swimming pool, sauna and jacuzzi	£200 per day

Catering

(All prices for one day.)	per person
Continental breakfast	£4.00
Half board – breakfast and evening meal	£9.00
Full board – three meals per day	£15.00
Morning coffee	£1.50
Tea and biscuits	£1.50
Full afternoon tea (with fresh pastries)	£3.50
Conference special banquet (please book at least one month ahead)	£25.00

Extra facilities

Coach transportation from the railway station (holds 52 persons)
Arrives at the station on the hour and half-past the hour.

Half-day service (8.00 – 13.00)	£175
Full-day service (8.00 – 21.00)	£400

Crèche facilities for children age three to ten years are available from 9.00 – 16.00 each day. Cost: £4.00 per child per day. MUST BE BOOKED WELL IN ADVANCE AS THERE IS A LIMITED NUMBER OF PLACES.

VAT at 17.5% will be added to all bills.

Audio-visual equipment may be reserved in advance at no extra charge.

All room prices include supervised car parking, 24-hour security, clean linen and room service, as well as a supply of tea and coffee in all standard and luxury rooms.

5.1 Bingo diaries

Teaching notes

To practise Arranging a meeting, discussing schedules, using time expressions and the present continuous for future arrangements.

Level Lower-intermediate and above.

Pre-experience learners As most of us make arrangements in everyday life, this activity shouldn't cause problems. Make sure that students are familiar with the vocabulary below.

Class size Multiples of four are ideal but twos and threes can do the activity too. (In this case, there may be one or two extra possible meeting times.)

One-to-one This is not ideal, but you can use the first and second diaries and look for three meeting times.

Potentially difficult vocabulary *negotiating*, *subsidiary*, *PR*, *strategy*, *trade fair*, *minutes* (for a meeting), *pay deal*, *draft* (verb), *pension scheme*, *invoice* (as verb and noun), *cocktail*, *quality control*

You will need Enough copies of all four **Diary** sheets (p59–62) to give one to each student in your class.

Procedure

This is a fairly controlled activity where students will tend to repeat certain structures. A good way to lead in to this activity, particularly with lower levels, is to revise prepositions of time. Useful ones would be **on** Thursday/at 4 pm/**between** 10.00 **and** 12.00/**up to** 3 pm/**before/after** 3 pm.

1 Elicit some ways to check someone's availability and put them on the board as a reminder. Expressions might include 'Are you free on ...?'/'What are you doing at ... on ...?'/'Could you make ...?/Would you be available for a meeting on ... at ...'

2 Put students into groups of four as far as possible, and hand a different diary to each student in the group. Allow students to read and absorb the game instructions at the top of their sheets. Encourage them to discuss the instructions in their group. If a group does not grasp the procedure, join the group and demonstrate briefly how the game works. Encourage higher level and/or more imaginative groups to expand on their queries, for example, 'You're flying to Athens ... Is that your first visit? I have heard that it's a very interesting city.'

3 While the groups play the game, note good and poor language use for feedback later. Check that students are not cheating by simply showing each other their schedules. Emphasize that this is a speaking activity, not a reading one.

4 When groups have finished, check whether they got the same days and times when they are all free. Encourage students to check any discrepancies.

5 Provide feedback on language used, or save it until next lesson as you think appropriate.

Person 1 Your diary for next week

Below is your diary for next week. You are going to be quite busy!

The other people in your group work for the same company as you but in different departments. You have to find two separate hours when you can all meet together.

Don't show your diary to the others, but find out by asking when they are free, for example, 'What are you doing on Thursday morning at 9.00, Han Yong?' or, 'Monika, are you free between 4.00 and 5.00 on Monday?'

As soon as you discover that one of you is not free, cross out that time in your diary. Continue to do this until you discover the two meeting times.

Time	Monday	Tuesday	Wednesday	Thursday	Friday
9.00–10.00	FREE	Business trip	FREE	Giving a presentation	Board meeting
10.00–11.00	Visiting a customer	Business trip	FREE	Giving a presentation	FREE
11.00–12.00	Visiting a customer	Business trip	Sales meeting	FREE	Negotiation
12.00–1.00 pm	Visiting a customer	Business trip	Sales meeting	FREE	Negotiation
1.00–2.00 pm	FREE	Business trip	FREE	Invoicing	FREE
2.00–3.00 pm	FREE	Business trip	Meet training officer	Invoicing	Departmental meeting
3.00–4.00 pm	Negotiation	Business trip	FREE	Meet telesales staff	Departmental meeting
4.00–5.00 pm	Negotiation	Business trip	Travel to Birmingham	Meet town mayor	Plan next week's schedule

Person 2 Your diary for next week

Below is your diary for next week. You are going to be quite busy!

The other people in your group work for the same company as you but in different departments. You have to find two separate hours when you can all meet together.

Don't show your diary to the others, but find out by asking when they are free, for example, 'What are you doing on Thursday morning at 9.00, Han Yong?' or, 'Monika, are you free between 4.00 and 5.00 on Monday?'

As soon as you discover that one of you is not free, cross out that time in your diary. Continue to do this until you discover the two meeting times.

Time	Monday	Tuesday	Wednesday	Thursday	Friday
9.00–10.00	Meeting	Meeting with sales director	Interviewing	Travelling	Board meeting
10.00–11.00	Meeting	FREE	Interviewing	Travelling	Prepare weekly financial report
11.00–12.00	Visiting a client	Meet PR manager	Interviewing	Travelling	Prepare weekly financial report
12.00–1.00 pm	Business lunch	Dentist's appointment (Urgent!)	FREE	Travelling	Plan next month's strategy
1.00–2.00 pm	Business lunch	German lesson	Seeing a customer	Travelling	FREE
2.00–3.00 pm	FREE	FREE	Seeing a customer	Travelling	Planning for Athens trip
3.00–4.00 pm	Factory visit	FREE	FREE	Return to the office	Fly to Athens
4.00–5.00 pm	Factory visit	Guest from Tunisia: tour of building	German lesson	FREE	Flying to Athens

Person 3 Your diary for next week

Below is your diary for next week. You are going to be quite busy!

The other people in your group work for the same company as you but in different departments. You have to find two separate hours when you can all meet together.

Don't show your diary to the others, but find out by asking when they are free, for example, 'What are you doing on Thursday morning at 9.00, Han Yong?' or, 'Are you free between 4.00 and 5.00 on Monday, Monika?'

As soon as you discover that one of you is not free, cross out that time in your diary. Continue to do this until you discover the two meeting times.

Time	Monday	Tuesday	Wednesday	Thursday	Friday
9.00–10.00	Out of the office	Fly to Edinburgh	FREE	FREE	Board meeting
10.00–11.00	Out of the office	Edinburgh (conference)	FREE	FREE	Prepare minutes from morning meeting
11.00–12.00	Out of the office	Edinburgh (conference)	Reporting on conference to MD	Feedback session with John Brown	Meeting MD to discuss restructuring
12.00–1.00 pm	Visit quality control consultant	Edinburgh (conference)	Interviewing job candidates	Business lunch	Local TV interview
1.00–2.00 pm	Invoicing	Edinburgh (conference)	Interviewing job candidates	Business lunch	FREE
2.00–3.00 pm	Invoicing	Edinburgh (conference)	Meet new PA	FREE	Travelling to London
3.00–4.00 pm	Preparing presentation for conference	Presentation in Edinburgh	FREE	FREE	Travelling to London
4.00–5.00 pm	Meeting chief accountant	Travel back from Edinburgh	Cocktails at The Elms Hotel (French guest)	FREE	Trade fair exhibition, London

Person 4 Your diary for next week

Below is your diary for next week. You are going to be quite busy!

The other people in your group work for the same company as you but in different departments. You have to find two separate hours when you can all meet together.

Don't show your diary to the others, but find out by asking when they are free, for example, 'What are you doing on Thursday morning at 9.00, Han Yong?' or, 'Monika, are you free between 4.00 and 5.00 on Monday?'

As soon as you discover that one of you is not free, cross out that time in your diary. Continue to do this until you discover the two meeting times.

Time	Monday	Tuesday	Wednesday	Thursday	Friday
9.00–10.00	Report writing	Prepare for discussion with MD	Negotiating a pay deal	PR event	Board meeting
10.00–11.00	Report writing	Prepare figures for discussion	Negotiating apay deal	PR event	Seeing a new client
11.00–12.00	Reports must be finished by 12.00	Pension scheme discussion with MD	Meet marketing director	PR event	Seeing a new client
12.00–1.00 pm	Counselling course	Pension scheme discussion	Meet marketing director	PR event: gala lunch	Local radio interview about a PR event
1.00–2.00 pm	Counselling course	Visitor from Indian subsidiary	FREE	Draft report on event	FREE
2.00–3.00 pm	Interviewing	Visitor from Indian subsidiary	Visit design office to see new adverts	Plan new publicity about new product	Check end of month accounting
3.00–4.00 pm	Interviewing	Reception for visitor	FREE	FREE	Accounting
4.00–5.00 pm	Decision about interviews candidates	Escort visitor to railway station	Plan details of PR event with organizer	Meet editor of local paper – give report	Present accounts to director

Teacher's master

Time	Monday	Tuesday	Wednesday	Thursday	Friday
9.00–10.00	1 FREE 2 Meeting 3 Out of the office 4 Report writing	1 Business trip 2 Meeting with sales director 3 Fly to Edinburgh 4 Prepare for discussion with MD	1 FREE 2 Interviewing 3 FREE 4 Negotiating a pay deal	1 Giving a presentation 2 Travelling 3 FREE 4 PR event	1 Board meeting 2 Board meeting 3 Board meeting 4 Board meeting
10.00–11.00	1 Visiting a customer 2 Meeting 3 Out of the office 4 Report writing	1 Business trip 2 FREE 3 Edinburgh (conference) 4 Prepare figures for discussion	1 FREE 2 Interviewing 3 FREE 4 Negotiating a pay deal	1 Giving a presentation 2 Travelling 3 FREE 4 PR event	1 FREE 2 Prepare weekly financial report 3 Prepare minutes from morning meeting 4 Seeing a new client
11.00–12.00	1 Visiting a customer 2 Visiting a client 3 Out of the office 4 Report must be finished by 12.00	1 Business trip 2 Meet PR manager 3 Edinburgh (conference) 4 Pension scheme discussion with MD	1 Sales meeting 2 Interviewing 3 Reporting on conference to MD 4 Meet marketing director	1 FREE 2 Travelling 3 Feedback session with John Brown 4 PR event	1 Negotiation 2 Prepare weekly financial report 3 Meeting MD to discuss restructuring 4 Seeing a new client
12.00–1.00 pm	1 Visiting a customer 2 Business lunch 3 Visit quality control consultant 4 Counselling course	1 Business trip 2 Dentist's appointment (Urgent!) 3 Edinburgh (conference) 4 Pension scheme discussion	1 Sales meeting 2 FREE 3 Interviewing job candidates 4 Meet marketing director	1 FREE 2 Travelling 3 Business lunch 4 PR event: gala lunch	1 Negotiation 2 Plan next month's strategy 3 Local TV interview 4 Local radio interview about a PR event
1.00–2.00 pm	1 FREE 2 Business lunch 3 Invoicing 4 Counselling course	1 Business trip 2 German lesson 3 Edinburgh (conference) 4 Visitor from Indian subsidiary	1 FREE 2 Seeing a customer 3 Interviewing job candidates 4 FREE	1 Invoicing 2 Travelling 3 Business lunch 4 Draft report on event	1 FREE 2 FREE 3 FREE 4 FREE
2.00–3.00 pm	1 FREE 2 FREE 3 Invoicing 4 Interviewing	1 Business trip 2 FREE 3 Edinburgh (conference) 4 Visitor from Indian subsidiary	1 Meet training officer 2 Seeing a customer 3 Meet new PA 4 Visit design office to see new adverts	1 Invoicing 2 Travelling 3 FREE 4 Plan new publicity about new product	1 Departmental meeting 2 Planning for Athens trip 3 Travelling to London 4 Check end of month accounting
3.00–4.00 pm	1 Negotiation 2 Factory visit 3 Preparing presentation for conference 4 Interviewing	1 Business trip 2 FREE 3 Presentation in Edinburgh 4 Reception for visitor	1 FREE 2 FREE 3 FREE 4 FREE	1 Meet telesales staff 2 Return to the office 3 FREE 4 FREE	1 Departmental meeting 2 Fly to Athens 3 Travelling to London 4 Accounting
4.00–5.00 pm	1 Negotiation 2 Factory visit 3 Meeting chief accountant 4 Decision about interviews	1 Business trip 2 Guest from Tunisia: tour of building 3 Travel back from Edinburgh 4 Escort visitor to railway station	1 Travel to Birmingham 2 German lesson 3 Cocktails at The Elms Hotel (French guest) 4 Plan details of PR event with organizer	1 Meet town mayor 2 FREE 3 FREE 4 Meet editor of local paper – give report	1 Plan next week's schedule 2 Flying to Athens 3 Trade fair exhibition, London 4 Present accounts to director

5.2 Napoleon's decision-making

Teaching notes

To practise Agreeing and disagreeing, giving an opinion and discussing a decision.

Level Upper-intermediate. The activity can be adapted for lower levels if the teacher simplifies the language of the **Worksheet** (p67) and provides a list of points for discussion in step three below.

Pre-experience learners Before starting, ask how far away your students would be prepared to work and for how long, in order to advance their careers.

Class size Four plus is best but two is possible if you add ideas.

One-to-one Possible, but is obviously less lively than with several students giving their opinions.

Overall timing 30–60 minutes, depending on the degree of student initiative.

Potentially difficult vocabulary *spouse, self-appraisal, relocating*

You will need One copy per student of the **Student instruction sheet** (p.65) with the 'Afterwards' sections cut off and set aside. Optional: One copy per student of the **Worksheet** (see stage two).

Procedure

1 Write 'Job Mobility' on the board and ask students what they understand this to mean. Elicit some ideas about the way the pattern of people's working lives have changed in the past ten to 15 years.

2 Hand out copies of the **Student instruction sheet** to students for them to read. Next, ask students to imagine that they are in the situation described on the sheet. Elicit from the class points which they think should be considered before a decision is made and write these on the board. (If students have real difficulty with this, some suggestions are family life, language, money, experience, stability, social life, the house, education for children, the spouse's job, and future prospects. Alternatively, you can hand out the **Worksheet** with its language prompts.)

3 Put students into pairs. If you do not use the **Worksheet**, ask one of the students to draw two columns on a sheet of paper, each headed *For* and *Against*. The pairs then discuss the points from the board and decide which column each one should go in; for example, the spouse's job – which would probably be difficult to obtain in the new country – might be in the *Against* column. Note that it may be possible for a point to go in both columns. Provide an appropriate time limit for your group.

4 When the time is up, ask the pairs to add up the total in each column and ring the one with the highest number. Then pairs join to make groups of four as far as possible (with a group of six if you have an extra pair). Hand out the *Afterwards* section and have the students discuss the questions.

5 A representative from each group tells the class about their decision. Encourage comments and debate.

Follow up

You could organize the class into groups of four or five to discuss the problem on the worksheet as a 'family role play'. Including a 'grandparent' (real or imagined) in the group will give the discussion a wider perspective.

Student instruction sheet

Situation

You have been hoping for promotion within your company for some time and in staff appraisal sessions you have had very positive feedback. The problem is that financial constraints have meant that there is very little mobility in the company; few people are leaving and almost no new jobs are being created. You have been considering looking for a higher level job elsewhere; however, you have suddenly been offered such a job in your firm's sister company abroad.

The company is in a country which is on a different continent and although English is used there as a second language, the first language of the country is one that you do not speak. The job, however, offers more responsibility in a developing market and would therefore be more exciting than your present one. The new job is much better paid than your current one and the company would pay relocation expenses if you accepted it. Your bosses have suggested that this career move would probably lead to an even better promotion later on. You know that this is probably the only opportunity you will have of gaining promotion within your company.

You are married and your spouse has a job here which s/he enjoys. You have two children aged 14 and 17 to support. Both the children are going to take important school exams within the next two years. You borrowed a large amount of money to buy your house, which you are still repaying. All of you have friends in the area and are members of local sports clubs.

Afterwards

Which column has the most points in it? Do you think this is the right decision? Compare your distribution of points with those of the other pair.

Napoleon is said to have used this method when making his decisions. How useful and objective do you think it is?

Be ready to summarize your discussion and tell the rest of the class about it.

Worksheet

spouse's job   culture   language

experience   money

contacts   stability   wider family

home

education   future prospects   health

status   colleagues

social life   travel   stress

FOR taking the job abroad	AGAINST taking the job abroad

5.3 How shall we market it?

Teaching notes

To practise Giving opinions, agreeing and disagreeing and reaching a group decision.

Level Mid-intermediate to advanced.

Pre-experience learners No special preparation needed. You may choose to spend a little longer on stage one.

Class size Two or more. The game is best played in threes or fours.

One-to-one Not ideal.

Overall timing 75–90 minutes.

Potentially difficult vocabulary *unisex, high interest* (account), *fuel consumption, reliable, charity, broad sheet, glossy magazine, leaflet, campaign, telesales*

You will need Per group of players, one copy of **Sheet one: Product descriptions**, p68, cut into five, one copy of **Sheet two: Game cards**, p69, cut into 20 cards and one copy of **Sheet three: Record of spending**, p70.

Procedure

1 Brainstorm ideas for gaining publicity and discuss which methods would be suitable for a consumer product and which for a service. Give a time limit.

2 Divide the class into groups of three or four and explain that they are going to discuss the best way to market five new products.

3 Demonstrate the game, using one group. Place the 'product' cards face down on the table between the students. Provide all 20 game cards if four students play and 15 if three play. A student shuffles the game cards and then deals them equally to the group so each student has five cards.

4 Choose one student to keep the **Record of spending** sheet.

5 Explain that the maximum each group can spend on marketing one product is 1,500 units. Each marketing method described on the **game cards** has a price in units.

6 The first student turns up the first 'product' card and shows or reads it to the others. They should then consider their cards and make one suggestion for a suitable marketing ploy, giving the reason for their choice, e.g.: 'I think that we should use local radio to advertise the new bank account because lots of business people listen to the radio at work.'

7 If the group agrees to the suggestion, it can be added to the **Record of spending** sheet. If not, the person must choose an alternative from their hand.

8 Each player must provide a minimum of one idea. After this, further ideas can be added if wished, as long as the spending limit is observed.

Note: If within budget, a group can choose to buy multiples of an idea, for example, ten radio adverts at two units each, costing 20 units. There is a column on the spending sheet for this. After the marketing mix has been decided for one product, the game cards are reshuffled and redistributed for the next product.

9 Provide each group with a set of game materials and monitor the activity, checking that the students are following the rules and noting their use of the target language.

10 When the groups have finished, ask a representative from each group to describe and explain its choices briefly for each product. (With confident groups, this can lead to inter-group debate continuing the use of language for agreeing and disagreeing!)

Feedback

If there is time, provide collated feedback from the notes you made during the game.

Possible follow up You could ask each group to prepare a short formal presentation of their marketing plan to give to the board of directors of the company which has created the product. The rest of the class can be the board and ask questions which they have. You could also get the students to produce pie charts showing the proportion of units spent on each method and get them to present them to the class.

Note: Teachers can devise their own product cards to make them relate to their students' professions when appropriate.

Sheet 1: Product descriptions

PRODUCT 1

Name of product/service:	*Gazelle*
Type of product/service:	Perfume spray for men or women.
Price range:	Medium to expensive
Intended market:	Higher paid professionals in their late 20s to mid-40s.
Special features?	It is unisex, has a fresh, 'wild' smell, which lasts a long time and is a product with an exclusive image.

PRODUCT 2

Name of product/service:	*Pro Per Cent*
Type of product/service:	A new high interest bank savings account.
Price range:	No charges if the customer abides by the rules of the account.
Intended market:	Investors, home owners and reliable savers age 40-plus.
Special features?	A guaranteed minimum percentage return on your investment which is 1% higher than other banks' offers.

PRODUCT 3

Name of product/service:	*Eno*
Type of product/service:	Small two-door car with low fuel consumption.
Price range:	Economy
Intended market:	First-time car buyers, young couples and single drivers.
Special features?	Comes in a wide range of bright colours. Optional sun roof and central locking (at extra cost).

PRODUCT 4

Name of product/service:	*Image Plus*
Type of product/service:	Wardrobe consultancy.
Price range:	Medium to expensive. Hourly rate charged to individual clients or package price for groups or companies.
Intended market:	Middle managers, professionals, particularly women age 25+.
Special features?	The service is individual and independent. It helps each person to develop a clear style for themselves. A follow-up service is offered as well as a purchase advisor to assist clients when they go clothes or accessory shopping.

PRODUCT 5

Name of product/service:	*Motorel*
Type of product/service:	Motel offering extra services for clients' cars.
Price range:	Economy to middle.
Intended market:	Travelling business people on a budget.
Special features?	Complete car valeting service available at a discount rate for clients of the motel. Minor repairs also undertaken. Room prices include breakfast and a guaranteed, protected garage space.

Sheet 2: Game cards

Special promotional hot air balloon to fly over the country and stop off to distribute leaflets and samples.
COST: 500 units

TV advert
COST per 10 seconds:
Morning broadcast: 100 units
4.00–6.00 pm broadcast: 150 units
8.00–11.00 pm broadcast: 250 units

Radio advert on light classical music station.
COST per 20 seconds: 50 units

Organizing a charity marathon race (with the new product name mentioned).
COST: 150 units

Advert in national broadsheet newspaper.
COST:
Weekday = 20 units
Weekend = 30 units

Leaflet campaign to one million households.
COST: 500 units

Charity fashion show featuring the new product/service.
COST: 200 units

Large poster campaign in all major cities.
COST: 1,000 units

Three days' large stand at a national trade exhibition.
COST: 35 units

Display in all the branches of a well-known department store.
COST: 300 units

Poster campaign on capital city's public transport, including underground stations, buses and trains.
COST: 1,000 units

Contribution to national children's charity. Cannot mention the product but it will give the company a positive image and provide reports on local radio and TV.
COST: Your choice, but a significant contribution would be 200+ units.

Hiring a well-known celebrity to promote the product for one year.
COST: 500 units

Employing telesales staff to contact potential customers and give out product information.
COST: 400 units for 6 months

Opening gala event for the product – with celebrity guests.
COST:
Capital city = 350 units
Industrial provincial city = 250 units
Large city which is an important cultural centre = 300 units

Advert in fortnightly trade magazines (e.g.: beauty and make up, banking and car owner magazines).
COST: 50 units per advert

Advert in weekly women's magazine (national distribution 250,000).
COST: Full page advert 50 units

Advert on back inside cover of these new books (sold at all major railway stations and airports):
1 The Psychology of Scent
2 Personal Finance: a guide
3 Car Maintenance
4 DIY Image Creation
5 Budget Travel Guide
COST: 250 units each book

Advert in monthly 'glossy' women's magazine.
COST:
half page = 150 units
full page = 250 units
double page = 350 units

Company representative interviewed on a national radio talk show.
COST: FREE if the product is not mentioned; 50 units if it is.

Sheet 3: Record of spending

	TYPE OF PUBLICITY	HOW MANY?	COST IN UNITS
P R O D U C T 1			
		Total cost:	
P R O D U C T 2			
		Total cost:	
P R O D U C T 3			
		Total cost:	
P R O D U C T 4			
		Total cost:	
P R O D U C T 5			
		Total cost:	

5.4 A meeting

Teaching notes

To practise The language of meetings, agreeing and disagreeing, asking for and giving opinions and reaching a compromise.

Level Upper-intermediate.

Pre-experience learners You may need to organize a pre-activity discussion about how a company can keep its workforce healthy and the importance of this in today's often stressful work environments.

Class size Four or more makes a good discussion, but you can attempt it with fewer.

One-to-one Although you could discuss the issues involved with your student, you will not have the variety of opinions of a group.

Overall timing About 60 minutes.

Potentially difficult vocabulary *subsidized, therapeutic (massage)*

You will need One copy of the **Worksheet** (p72) per student.

Procedure

Lead in (optional): This activity can be used either to follow on from material on the language of meetings or as a 'one off' activity. Decide firstly whether the students need to be reintroduced to the appropriate phrases to use in meetings or not. If they do, a quick way to elicit these is to draw a table on the board with functional headings such as 'Introducing Ideas', 'Agreeing and Disagreeing', 'Changing the topic', etc. Prepare some cards with phrases to go under these headings, hand them out randomly and let students put their cards under the appropriate heading. (Cards can be rearranged as necessary.) Alternatively, let students add their own phrases to the board and encourage self- and peer correction.

1 Tell students they are going to organize a meeting among themselves. Explain that they are all directors of a company and have to make a decision about how to spend an amount of money set aside for reducing employees' stress levels. If you have a large class, divide it into two or three groups. Ask a chairperson to volunteer, or for the group to choose one. Then hand out copies of the **Worksheet** and give a time limit for students to read it and make their own notes if they wish.

2 Before starting on discussion, decide on a method of gathering material for feedback. You could record or videotape the meeting or simply write notes of your own as you listen. The first two methods allow students to check their own performance, but a less confident group may be discouraged to listen to or watch an error-ridden recording. You could consult students beforehand on the method they would prefer. Only speak yourself during the meeting if things break down irrevocably. The whole point of the activity is that it is student-led.

3 Ask the chairperson to open the meeting and to ensure that s/he keeps the discussion balanced, allows everyone a chance to give their opinion and keeps to the agreed time limit. Thirty-five to forty-five minutes is a reasonable limit.

4 As the meeting closes, the chairperson summarizes the decision made and reasons for it.

5 Decide whether to give feedback immediately or later, but remember that immediate criticism can destroy a good atmosphere if the discussion has gone well.

Follow up

Students can consider the different roles they took in the discussion and why. Mixed nationality groups can compare the different approaches of their colleagues.

Worksheet

You are the senior managers of a large consulting company which employs approximately 400 people. Last year staff absences due to stress-related illnesses cost the company £90,000. You have a budget of £200,000 to spend over the next three years on reducing staff stress levels. You must make a decision during this meeting as the managing director must report your suggestions to the board of directors tomorrow.

When discussing the options below, consider:

1 How many employees could benefit.

2 The physical and mental health advantages.

3 How long the benefits might last.

Note: All costs include any initial investment plus running costs for three years.

WELL COMPANY PLAN

PROVISION	COST
Build and maintain a small multi-gym in the company. (Fifteen people at once.)	£200,000
Build a medium-sized swimming pool in the company. (Twenty-five people at once.)	£200,000
Off-site weekend stress management course for 50 employees.	£50,000
On-site doctor available in the company 2.5 days per week.	£90,000
On-site dental surgeon available half a day per week.	£30,000
On-site therapeutic masseur one day per week.	£36,000
On-site professional counsellor one day per week.	£36,000
Training a volunteer employee as a counsellor, to work 2.5 days per week.	£50,000
Hire of local sports hall one evening per week for team games (two large halls from 5.30 pm to 10.00 pm).	£15,000
Hire of local swimming pool four hours per week for employees.	£40,000
Introduction of subsidized healthy options in the staff canteen.	£150,000
Introduction of flexitime for all workers.	£20,000
Providing ten special rooms in the company where staff can relax in their breaks with comfortable furniture, newspapers, plants, etc.	£100,000

6.1 Conditionals in a negotiation

Teaching notes

To practise Forming different conditional sentences used in a negotiation and recognizing appropriate usage of different conditional forms.

Level Upper-intermediate plus.

Pre-experience learners No special preparation needed.

Class size Six plus is ideal.

One-to-one This can be used as a table-top matching-and-ordering activity.

Overall timing 30 minutes.

Potentially difficult vocabulary *bulk buying*

You will need One set of the **Cards** on the next page (74), cut up and (optional) one whole copy for each student.

Procedure

1 Write these sentences on the board and ask students which one would be most likely to be used by a customer, and which by a salesperson:

A: 'If you agree to our offer, we'll deliver free of charge.'

B: 'If you lowered your price, we'd accept your offer.'

A is the salesperson and B the customer, firstly because of what they say but also because of the way they say it. Often, the first conditional sounds more persuasive because it suggests that the action is more likely to happen; the second conditional sounds less likely and expresses more caution. Elicit as much of this as you can from your students. Tell students that they are going to put together a dialogue of two people negotiating purchase terms.

2 Seat half the class opposite the other half, in two rows. Hand out the first six shaded cards and the last six unshaded cards to one side, then the remaining cards to the other side. The cards should be shared out among the students on that side. Explain that each exchange in the dialogue starts with a

shaded card. Ask one side to start by a student reading out a shaded card. The other side should respond by finding the right ending. Everyone should be encouraged to correct and assist. Next, the other side starts with a shaded card and the process continues until all the pairs have been found. Students then arrange the dialogue in order. Encourage students to read aloud sections as they put the dialogue together to check whether it sounds correct.

3 Give feedback on the order of dialogue chosen by the students, discussing who is speaking in which part of the dialogue and getting students to identify the types of conditional used in each case and what their effect is. Provide each student with a copy of the whole dialogue if you wish.

Large class alternative procedure: If you have a class of 24 or more, you could give each student one card, then ask pairs to find each other. Finally ask the pairs to arrange themselves into a line in the order of the dialogue. (If you have more than 24 students, let some students share a card.)

Cards

If you can offer us a special discount ...	... we may be able to sign the contract early.
Sign the contract today ...	... and we'll give you an extra 10% discount.
If we couldn't sign the contract today ...	... would you still be able to offer a discount later on?
Well, we usually only offer an extra discount ...	... when clients sign the same day.
To take a different approach ... If we were thinking of ordering in bulk	... would you have anything to offer in the way of a reduction?
Yes, if you order more than 1,000 items at once ...	... we will give you 5% off.
And if we ordered 10,000 at once ...	... we could expect free delivery, right?
If you place such a large order ...	... we'll give free delivery and the option of our super express service which arrives in 36 hours.
Last year, if products were ordered direct from you ...	... you offered a one-year guarantee. Is that still so?
Yes, in fact if you place your order by the end of the week ...	... you'll be offered a special one-year guarantee on all the products you buy.
OK, to sum up, if we sign a contract for 10,000 today ...	... you will give us a 10% discount for signing today, a 5% discount for the large order, free delivery with super express option and a one-year guarantee on the goods. Is that right?
Yes. If you just give us a moment ...	... we'll prepare all the papers for you to sign.

6.2 Someone else's shoes

Teaching notes

To practise The language of negotiating, recognizing the other party's position and being sensitive to it, evaluating one's own performance in a negotiation. The activity can be successfully used for awareness-building prior to examining the language of negotiation.

Level Mid-intermediate and above.

Pre-experience learners No special requirements.

Class size Any even number. An 'extra' student could act as an observer for one pair.

One-to-one This is not recommended for one-to-one classes as it is based on the assumption of linguistic parity.

Overall timing 80–90 minutes.

Potentially difficult vocabulary *wholesale, dealing in bulk, discount*

You will need Enough copies of **Sheets one and two** (p76) so that each student has either A or B, and enough of **Sheet three** part one and **Sheet four** part two (p78–79) for each student to have one.

Procedure

1 Draw a mind map on the board with 'the good negotiator' written in the centre, then get students to brainstorm adjectives that describe a good negotiator. Either you or the students then add these to the mind map. Now explain that the students are going to try out a negotiation.

2 Divide the class into two. Give one half the **Role A cards** and the other half the **Role B cards**. Let all the As and Bs read through the instructions. Make it clear that the B people, from a developing country, are selling their products to the As, from a developed country.

3 Assign each A student a B partner and ask them to start the role play. Observe students' role play styles and make notes on good and poor language usage as well as body language.

4 Ensure that the students have enough time to be able to try out their role and assess a suitable point at which to ask for silence. This should not be when the students have reached the end of their negotiation as the point of the exercise is to get them to reflect on their participation in the role play while they are still in the middle of it. Immediately hand out copies of **Sheet three**: part one to each student and ask them to fill it in. Help where necessary.

5 When the students have filled in the form, ask students to swap role play cards and continue the negotiation, taking their partner's role. They can use their notes that they have just made to help them to carry on from where their partner left off. Make notes for yourself as in stage three above.

6 Allow students as long as you feel is appropriate (perhaps a little longer than in the first section) then stop them, hand out Part two and ask them to fill it in.

7 Now ask students to compare sheets three and four and discuss their reactions to the activity.

8 Make sure that you allow plenty of time for this stage as it is vital to students' understanding of the negotiating process that they have been trying out. Ask each pair to tell you and the class how the activity made them feel about the negotiating process. Invite comments from the rest of the class. You could also refer them back to the adjectives from the initial brainstorming and see how students think they measured up as negotiators.

Feedback

Provide brief feedback from your notes taken in stages three and five above, reinforcing positive examples of good negotiating where you can.

Note: This activity primarily provides the opportunity to examine the negotiating process and what it feels like to step into another person's shoes, so I suggest that you do not focus on language errors during it.

Sheet one: role A

You are an ...

international sales manager for a large shoe manufacturing company in a developed country.

You should negotiate ...

the size of the first order to supply to person B's company (in a developing country) and the price.

The product ...

good quality leather men's and women's shoes in standard styles (not high fashion).

Normal wholesale price = U.S. **$40** a pair.

Points to bear in mind ...

★ You are visiting your partner's country; you are a guest there.

★ You know that inflation is very high in this country and the local currency is weak.

★ Your company has warned you about the risk of being too generous when dealing with a developing country. Recently it has lost quite a lot of money in this way.

★ You would like a minimum order of **10,000** pairs and a maximum of **50,000**.

★ The normal credit period for payment of goods is two months from the delivery date but you can extend this to three months if necessary.

★ You can give a discount of **8%** on an order of **20,000** pairs or more and **3.5%** on an order of between **10** and **20,000** pairs. (These are the terms for any customer.)

Note: This is your best contact in this country and your partner's firm has a good reputation. You must try to get some sort of deal.

Sheet one: role B

You are ...

the import manager for a large private import-export company in a country which does not have hard currency and which has only been importing goods from hard currency countries for a short time.

You should negotiate ...

the size of the first order from a big western manufacturer and the price of the goods.

The product ...

good quality leather men's and women's shoes in standard styles (not high fashion). This type of quality is not yet available in your country.

Normal wholesale price = U.S. **$25** a pair.

Points to bear in mind ...

★ Negotiations are taking place in your country; your partner is a guest.

★ Your partner is the sales manager for the western country.

★ You know that westerners often see your country as very unstable economically and that that might make them unsure about doing business with firms there.

★ Your country has a lot of potential as a new market and the economy has improved a lot recently.

★ You would like to place a bulk order for **100,000** pairs of shoes if possible, as you deal in bulk and that is your normal size order.

★ You hope for a **15–20%** discount on such a big order and need a minimum of 8 weeks' credit from the date that the goods are delivered. This is because the distribution network in your country is still rather ineffective and slow due to transport and other problems.

Note: This is the best opportunity you have had so far to do large scale business with the developed market. You must try to get some sort of deal.

Sheet three: Part one

The main points which my partner made:

....

....

....

....

....

....

....

....

....

....

....

....

At the beginning of the discussion I felt that:

I was in a stronger position. ☐

I was in a weaker position than my partner. ☐

We were more or less equal. ☐

We were moving towards a compromise. ☐

Just before we were asked to stop, I felt that:

I was in a stronger position. ☐

I was in a weaker position than my partner. ☐

We were more or less equal. ☐

We were moving towards a compromise. ☐

(Tick one box)

Sheet four: Part two

Playing my partner's role was*:

> impossible   very difficult   difficult

> quite easy   easy   no problem at all

(*Circle one word)

Did you notice anything about changing roles which surprised or interested you? Write here:

....

....

....

....

....

....

....

....

....

....

....

Just before we were asked to stop, I felt that:

My partner was in a stronger position.	☐	My partner was in a weaker position.	☐
We were more or less equal.	☐	We were more or less equal.	☐
We achieved a compromise.	☐	We were moving towards a compromise.	☐

(Tick one box)

7.1 The crystal ball game

Teaching notes

To practise Using the future forms *will* and *going to* to discuss future possibilities and changes and make predictions.

Level Lower-intermediate and above.

Pre-experience learners This activity is based on the students' knowledge of each other from working in class, so no special preparation is needed.

Class size Three or more. The teacher should be part of the class for this activity. You could try it with two students, but it may be a bit too intimate.

One-to-one This is not a suitable activity for such classes but you could try asking the student to write you a prediction and you write the student one. You could read them in private and reply in writing or by recording your comments onto tape.

Overall timing This depends on the size, level and openness of the class. As a rough guide, allow five minutes per student for predictions.

You will need To clear any tables to the side of the room and set out a ring of chairs – one each for the students and you.

Note: This activity is best suited to students who have already got to know each other, as it is quite a personal activity. The closer the group is, the better the activity will work. (I have mostly used this activity at the end of courses.)

Procedure

1 Do a quick revision session on when we use *will* and *going to*. Make sure that students understand the idea of intent and control of circumstances with *going to* and the lack of them when *will* is used to make a prediction.

2 Sit in a ring with your students. Hold out your hands as though you are holding a largish ball. Explain that you are holding a crystal ball which helps people to see the future and that they are going to make predictions about the other students in the class. Choose a student and make a couple of predictions about them, e.g. 'I think that Renato will work very hard next year and will probably get promotion in his office. Maybe he will also marry an Italian woman and have lots of children!' Emphasize your use of *will* because you cannot be sure and you do not control the situation you are talking about.

3 Explain that the student whose future is being 'predicted' must wait until s/he has heard all the predictions before s/he can answer. Meanwhile, hand the 'ball' to a student. The only person who speaks is the person with the 'ball'. Encourage each student to make at least one prediction, then invite the student whose future is being discussed to tell the class how likely it is that the predictions will come true. For example, Renato might respond, 'I hope that I will get promotion next year and I am sure that I will work hard because we have a new project coming up at work. But I am almost certain that I will not get married, because my lifestyle is too unsettled.'

4 Invite the students to continue in the same way until everyone, including you, has been given predictions and the chance to reply to them.

Feedback

It is not recommended that a formal feedback session is given after this activity as it will break the atmosphere of trust created by doing it. However, you could encourage peer correction during it and/or offer reformulated versions of inaccurate utterances.

Follow up

If you are using this activity at the end of a course, you could distribute a class list of addresses and invite students to write to you in English telling you whether the predictions came true or not. If enough students do this, you could send out a mini 'class newsletter' to them containing the responses.

7.2 A company's progress

Teaching notes

To practise Describing a line graph and presenting information.

Level Upper-intermediate/intermediate with preparation.

Pre-experience learners It would be useful to have a discussion about the type of problems a small company starting in business may encounter in the first few years.

Class size Two plus.

One-to-one This is not a suitable activity.

Overall timing 30 minutes.

Potentially difficult vocabulary *market share, brand name, soya, to pay off a loan, launch* (a campaign), *quality control*

You will need One copy each of **Sheet A** (p82) for half the students in your class and one copy each of **Sheet B** (p83) for the other half of the class.

Procedure

1 Tell students that they are going to look at and discuss the progress of a small dairy products company which started in business ten years ago.

2 Give half your students sitting on one side of the class **Sheet B**. Give **Sheet A** to the others. All the student As should work together and the student Bs likewise. If you have a very large class, further divide each half into two more halves. Emphasize that they will be making educated guesses at this stage. Encourage the use of appropriate vocabulary. For example, student A might say, 'There was a rise in the fourth and fifth years, so maybe they introduced a new product' or student B might say, 'There should be a fairly sharp increase after they introduce some new products'.

3 When student As have produced some points and student Bs have produced their rough graphs, pair up each A student with a B student. Have them discuss and compare their results. They should then add the factor numbers from **Sheet B** to the appropriate places on **Sheet A**.

4 Draw the graph in large scale on the board or use a copied OHT. Ask representatives from the pairs to describe a slot of time in as much detail as they can, giving reasons for any changes which take place within that time slot. Students can use the information on **Sheet B** together with their own ideas, which might be based on experience.

Follow up

Ask students to prepare a graph on a different topic, such as how they feel their English has improved since they started (many students, for instance, reach plateaux of learning at certain stages). Alternatively students might like to depict how their energy levels go up and down on a typical working day, or over a week. If students work for the same company or department, they might be prepared to discuss its progress. (However, you need to check whether this would be acceptable before suggesting it.)

Sheet A

Look at the company's profits over ten years. With the other student As, suggest why the variations occurred. Note your ideas at suitable points on the graph.

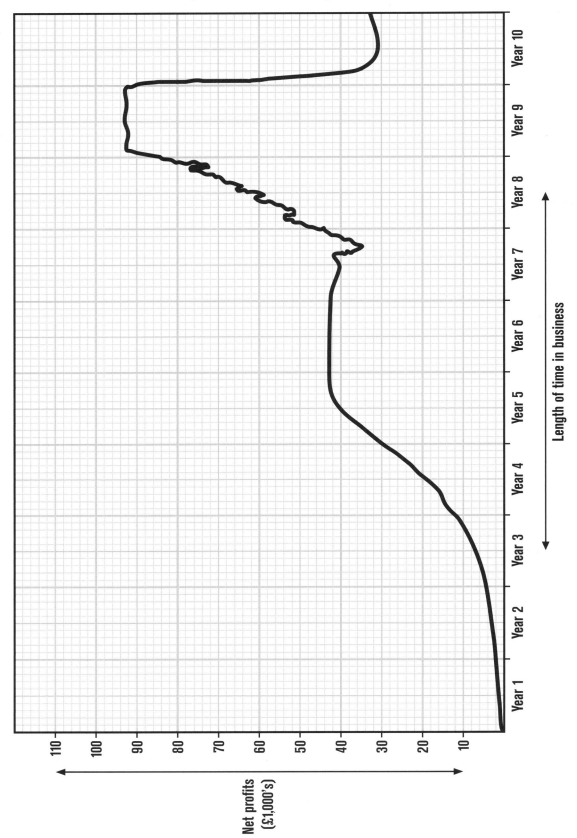

Sheet B

Here are some factors which influenced a dairy food company's first ten years of business. It is a small firm which distributes its goods mainly through supermarkets. Read the information below and sketch a rough graph of how you would predict the company's profits to increase or decrease over the ten years. Use the vertical axis for profit and the horizontal axis for time.

FACTORS AFFECTING BUSINESS

1 Bank loans taken out to start the business had to be paid off early on.

2 Not much could be spent on marketing at first.

3 Later on, the company launched a successful marketing campaign to get its brand name recognized.

4 They also introduced some new products.

5 Factors three and four resulted in the company obtaining a steady market share.

6 Some competitors aggressively challenged the company's market share but did not succeed in seriously affecting a period of rapid growth.

7 A period of stability followed this, during which the company could rely on its, by now, well-known, brand name.

8 A nationwide health scare about one of the company's best-selling cheeses caused the worst decline in the company's history.

9 The company's response was the introduction of much stricter quality controls.

10 It also started to sell a new range of healthy alternatives to dairy products, made of soya.

7.3 Graph dictations

Teaching notes

To practise The language of change in describing line graphs. This activity can be used as part of an exercise on making presentations.

Level Lower-intermediate and above. Higher level students may not need to use **Sheet one** (p85). In this case, stages one to three in the procedure can be omitted.

Pre-experience learners Pre-teach the topic of graphs as used in business. Try using some authentic material from the financial press.

Class size Two or more. The teacher can form a pair with a remaining student.

One-to-one Yes.

Overall timing 35–45 minutes.

Potentially difficult vocabulary *fluctuate, decline, slump, suddenly, steadily*

You will need One copy of **Sheet one**, cut up, which the whole class can use, plus one copy of **Sheet two** (p86) per pair of students, cut into two as indicated.

Procedure

1 Divide the class into two groups. Give Group A the five graphs from **Sheet one** and Group B the five written descriptions. Ask Group A to write brief written descriptions. Group B should draw rough line graphs, illustrating the descriptions.

2 When this is done, swap Group A's original five graphs with group B's five written descriptions. Have the students match the new originals with their descriptions or rough graphs.

3 Finally, merge the groups. Distribute all ten original items and ask students to pair up the graphs with the written descriptions. Check any comprehension problems at this stage.

4 Students now work in pairs but should not be able to see their partner's sheet.

5 Give one student in each pair a copy of the top half of **Sheet two** and the other student the bottom half. Students unfamiliar with this sort of activity may need some demonstration first. Emphasize that the students should not show their sheet to their partner until they have completed the activity. As you observe this activity, take notes on students' use of the target language.

6 Finally, ask students to compare their completed versions and the originals and to report back briefly on how close they were.

Feedback

Give feedback immediately. Remember to start with some positive comments before giving constructively critical ones.

Follow up

There are a number of possible activities that you could use in the lessons that follow:

1 Students draw a graph illustrating a development at work or in their country and dictate it to the rest of the class.

2 Record a financial report from the radio which could be fairly easily represented in graph form. Then get students to fill in an empty graph with suitably labelled axes prepared by you. A tapescript for checking is a good idea.

3 Copy some graphs from e.g. the financial pages of a newspaper. You, or a student, describes one of the graphs and the others identify as quickly as possible which one it is.

Sheet one

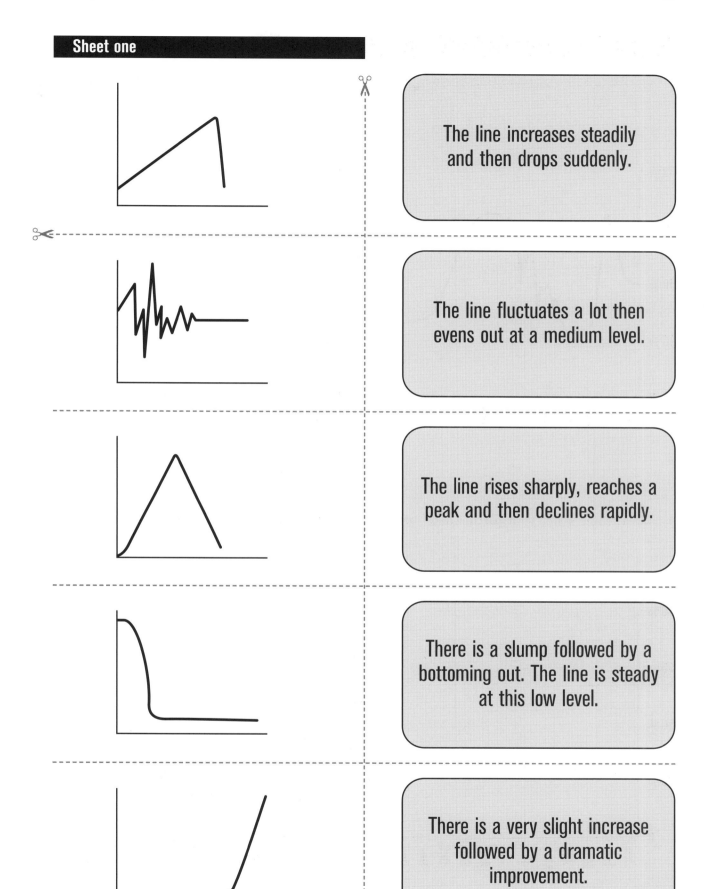

The line increases steadily and then drops suddenly.

The line fluctuates a lot then evens out at a medium level.

The line rises sharply, reaches a peak and then declines rapidly.

There is a slump followed by a bottoming out. The line is steady at this low level.

There is a very slight increase followed by a dramatic improvement.

Sheet two

1 Describe this line graph to your partner.

2 Draw the line which your partner describes.

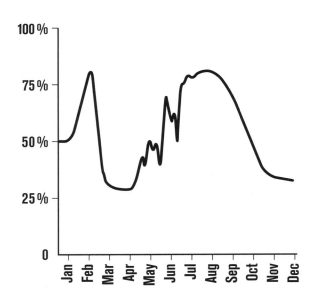

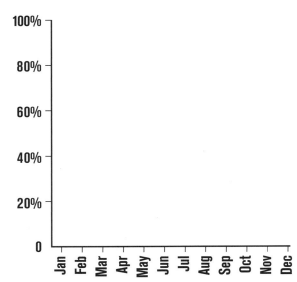

✂ -

1 Draw the line which your partner describes.

2 Describe this line graph to your partner.

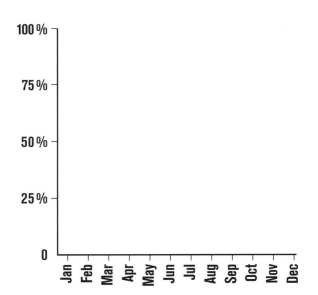

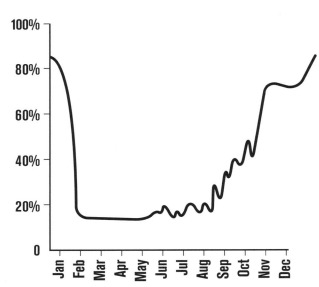

8.1 Describe an organigram

Teaching notes

To practise Describing a company's structure and jobs using the language of relative position, e.g.: *senior to, reports to*.

Level Intermediate and above.

Pre-experience learners Ask learners to describe a company they know well. Alternatively, provide them with organizational charts to describe.

One-to-one Yes. The teacher can draw the diagram dictated by the student and vice versa,

if the teacher works for an organization. Otherwise use another company's organizational chart from its brochure.

Class size Two plus.

Overall timing 50–80 minutes.

You will need Sufficient pencils, erasers and blank or squared paper for all students in your class.

Procedure

1 Introduce the topic of organizational charts or organigrams, perhaps by drawing one of the organization you work for (if you are not in a one-to-one class) and describing it. Ask students if they think organizations' shapes have changed recently; for example, many have cut down on middle management and become a flatter shape.

2 Now put the key words *shape?* *layers?* and *job titles?* on the board and ask students to draw a diagram of the company they work for, or, in the case of very large organizations, the department or section. Check students' work and help out where necessary. (This can be done as self-study if you wish.) Students should not show their diagram to others.

3 Pair students up, or if you have a large class, put students into groups of four. Now in turn, each student dictates her/his chart to the other student(s). The person dictating should be as clear as possible. Draw students' attention to the key words on the board as features which should be described early on. For example, 'My company has basically four layers to it and it's a triangular or pyramid shape. There is one person at the top, that's the CEO; five in the second layer – they are the senior managers for each department, etc.'

4 The other students should be encouraged to ask questions and demand clarification to check what they are drawing. They may compare their efforts as they go along. The person dictating should not, however, look at their versions until the end. As you listen, note any good phrases or words used, as well as any recurring language problems. Intervene as little as possible, as this is a student-led activity.

5 When the dictation is finished, students compare their drawing with the speaker's original and discuss any differences. Then roles are swapped around, and a new student describes her/his organigram, proceeding as above.

6 Provide brief feedback on the language used during the activity, encouraging peer correction of any errors.

7 With interested learners, follow up with comparisons and discussion of company structures, hierarchies and division of responsibilities.

8 If you have time, prepare large scale versions of your students' organigrams to put up on the walls.

8.2 Talking pictures

Teaching notes

To practise The language of description and speculation, asking for and giving opinions, agreeing and disagreeing.

Level Intermediate.

Pre-experience learners No special requirements.

Class size Two plus.

One-to-one This is possible but will demand a lot of the student. The teacher could look at a different picture from the student's and both could do the brainstorming below (stage one).

Overall timing 30–40 minutes.

You will need In a small class, one photo of a business person per student (see pp89–90). In a larger class, pairs or threes should all have different photos to look at which are then rotated around the groups. One photo of your own.

Procedure

1 Hold up your own photo and ask students to guess who the person might be, what s/he does, where s/he lives, what s/he is like, etc. Praise students who use the modal/ verbs of possibility such as *may*, *might* and *could*. If you are using your own personal photo, tell the students who the person really is, once they have exhausted possibilities.

2 Give pairs or threes the same photo to share. They look at it and brainstorm ideas about who the person is, what s/he does, where s/he lives, what sort of person s/he is, etc. Encourage the use of modals again. A representative should make notes on her/ his group's ideas. If they run short of ideas, ask them to consider what might have happened just before the picture was taken and what might happen afterwards. Provide a time limit for this activity and its repetitions (in stage three below).

3 Next, each pair/ three passes their photo round to the next group, so that each group has a new photo to look at. The process in stage two is repeated with this photo. Once the time limit is reached, the photos are passed on again, until each group has had a chance to look at all of the photos.

4 Put each photo in turn on the board and invite a representative from each group to summarize their group's comments on it. Alternate the representatives as you discuss the subsequent photos.

5 Give feedback on the language used in the discussions, remembering to include positive as well as negative observations. If you are short of time, you could save this stage for next lesson, using one of the techniques described in the **Giving feedback** section of this book.

Follow up

Ask students to write up the ideas from their discussions. If you teach in a room where the walls can be decorated, display the final drafts of their work, mounted, next to the photographs.

8.3 My working day

Teaching notes

To practise Describing a work routine, asking simple questions about someone else's work routine, e.g. *How long do you spend each day doing X?* and making comparisons using *more*, *less* and the gerund, e.g. *My partner spends less time using the computer than me.*

Level Elementary to mid-intermediate. Also a 'get to know you' activity for higher levels, but reduce the times indicated.

Pre-experience learners Adjust for these learners. Full-time students could discuss study habits; part-time students consider their domestic routine and how their study fits into it.

Class size Two or more.

One-to-one Yes. The teacher acts as the student's partner.

Overall timing 35–55 minutes.

Potentially difficult vocabulary for elementary students: *to spend time (+ ing)*, *the least*, *most*; phrases connected with students' work, e.g. telephoning phrases, language relating to using a computer and having meetings.

You will need One copy of the **Worksheet** (p92) per student plus some spare pencils for those students and a few erasers. (It is often necessary for students to adjust their charts.)

Procedure

1 Tell students they are going to find out how hard their colleagues work! Hand out **Worksheets** to everyone and pair students.

2 Elicit questions that students could ask to fill in the chart for their partner. Use **1** on the sheet to get them started.

3 Demonstrate how to fill in the pie chart. Ask a student a question and shade in and label the appropriate amount of the chart.

4 Ask students to write their partner's name on their **Worksheet** and then start the interview described in **1** in order to fill in the pie chart. When one pie chart is complete, the students change roles so the person who was answering becomes the questioner. Take

notes on good language use and any common errors, especially with the structure *spend time doing*.

5 When students finish, ask them to quickly compare their partner's chart and their own. Next, get them to complete the gap fill sentences in **2**. Go around the class and help where necessary.

6 When all the students have completed **2**, assign them a new partner and ask them to show that partner the pie chart they produced and the sentences in **2**. If you have a very small class, discuss the charts and sentences together.

Feedback

Praise good examples of language that you noted during stage four above and present any common errors. See if the students can guess how those errors could be improved. With elementary students, you may like to take their worksheets in at the end to check.

Note: This activity can also be used as a way of finding out how much time students spend using English normally, and the way they use it, e.g. telephoning, speaking face to face, writing letters, etc. for needs analysis.

Follow up

1 You could follow up this with a 'whole class' activity. Students work out the class averages of time spent at work and spent doing different things. This would be useful for a group which needs to be able to use simple mathematical terms in English, or to talk about statistics in a presentation.

2 You could also collect in the charts and blank out the names with paper. Display with charts on the walls at the next lesson. Then ask students to go around and guess to whom the charts refer.

Worksheet

Your partner's name ....

1 Ask your partner about his or her working day, for example: '**How many hours a day do you spend talking on the phone?**' Fill in and label the chart to show the answers. If your partner's working day is eight hours, fill in eight of the sections, but you could also ask such questions as '**How long do you spend travelling to and from work?**'

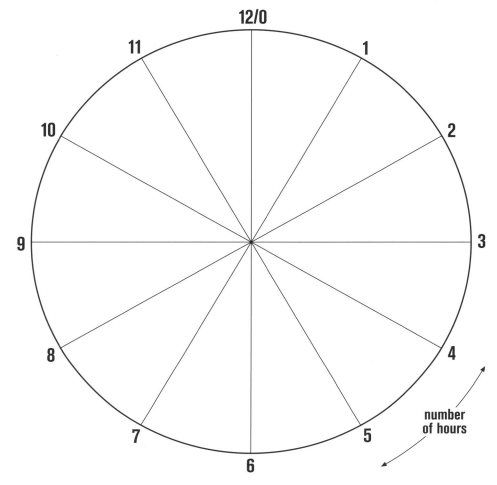

2 When you have finished the chart, fill in the gaps in these sentences:

a My partner spends most of his/her time .... ing.

b S/he spends the least time .... ing.

c My partner spends more time .... ing than
.... ing.

d My partner spends more time .... ing than me at work.

e My partner spends less time .... than me.

9.1 A roof over your head?

Teaching notes

To practise Recognizing the key words for describing a process (buying property in the UK) and using them to put a description in order.

Level Upper-intermediate and above.

Pre-experience learners No special problems, but property-buying practices vary from country to country.

Class size Four plus ideally.

One-to-one Yes. In stage three below, take all the beginnings of the sentences, sit opposite your student and read them aloud, as suggested. Your student can spread out the endings and choose a response. Stage four is done by the student alone. Once s/he has decided the order s/he is happy with, compare it with the original. Discuss differences. Alternatively, share out beginnings and endings so that you have half of each type (both ensure that neither of you has matching pairs). This reduces the student's workload.

Potentially difficult vocabulary *solicitor (US lawyer), mortgage, insurance, valuation report, deposit (US down payment) move in*

Timing 45–60 minutes.

You will need Three copies of the **Worksheet** (p94) cut up into strips. Divide one of the sets of strips into two piles, with equal numbers of the unshaded and shaded strips in each. Ensure that there are no matching pairs in either pile.

Note: If you are teaching in a context in which it is not common for people to purchase their own home, consider missing out stage two below.

Procedure

1 Tell students they will examine the process of buying a flat or house. First, find out what they think about buying property. Students discuss the following questions in pairs. Give a time limit. Then get brief feedback from each pair.

1 *What are the advantages and disadvantages of buying your own place to live?*

2 *Do you own, or do you want to own your own place to live in? Why /Why not?*

2 As a class, brainstorm the stages of buying property. Put suggestions on the board and encourage peer correction.

3 Now tell the class that they are going to work with a description of this process in the UK. Put them into Teams A and B and organize the classroom so that the teams face each other. Hand out one pile of 'half statements' to one team and the remainder to the other. Tell them that the shaded strips are the 'beginnings' and the unshaded strips are the 'endings'.

4 Team A now reads aloud a 'beginning' strip. Team B consults to find the correct ending, then reads this aloud in response. Give a time limit for consultation. If Team B gets the answer right first time, they are awarded a mark. If not, point out the correct answer. No mark is given.

5 Next, Team B reads a 'beginning' strip and the game proceeds in this way. Encourage students to work cooperatively and consult each other. When all the sentences are used up, give the score for each team.

6 Now hand each team a new set of strips and ask them to order them correctly. (This will involve both revising the pairings students have just completed, and spotting the 'clues' or language markers that indicate how to order the sequence.) Give a time limit for this stage.

7 Check the teams' texts. One way to do this is to ask one team to read their final version aloud, while the other team listens and intervenes when their version is different. Alternatively read the correct version, and invite queries if a team's version differs from yours.

8 Now compare the points on the board from stage two with the strip text. Further interesting cultural comparisons might be made at this point if the country you are working in has very different systems for home-buying.

Worksheet

Find out from us how much you are able to borrow;

If the valuation report is satisfactory and you have received a mortgage offer from us,

this will help you establish the price range you can afford.

your solicitor will arrange for you to sign the purchase contract and will ask you for a deposit.

Start looking for the property you want

Once the seller has signed an identical copy of the contract, and you have agreed the completion date when you will move in,

within your price range.

your solicitor will exchange contracts with the seller's solicitor

Once you have found your ideal home,

and your deposit will be passed to the seller.

make an offer to the seller.

Before completion, your solicitor will ask you to

If your offer is accepted,

sign the necessary legal documents and will obtain the cheque for your mortgage from us.

contact us to complete the mortgage application papers.

Your solicitor will complete the purchase and

Contact your solicitor and

arrange for the keys to be given to you.

advise her or him of your intention to purchase the property.

The property is now yours.

9.2 The process jigsaw

Teaching notes

To practise Describing processes, using and recognizing key words marking stages of a process e.g. *next, finally,* and referential words, e.g. *this, that.*

Level Mid-intermediate and above. See note at end for lower levels.

Pre-experience learners No special preparation.

Class size Two plus. (Do in twos/threes.) But in a class of two students, stage two is worked on individually.

One-to-one Work with the student. Allow the student to take the initiative and produce your own jigsaw in stage two.

Overall timing Part one: 35–45 minutes; Part two: 50–75 minutes. Total: 85–120 minutes. (Parts one and two can be carried out in different lessons.)

Potentially difficult vocabulary *essential requirements, to shortlist, to eliminate, desirable* (qualities for a job), *a* (company) *policy, to fulfil criteria*

You will need For each pair/three in your class: one copy of **Sheets one**, **two** and **three** (pp96–8), and prepare some blank A4 card and a class set of scissors.Cut up **Sheets one** and **two** and keep each set in a labelled envelope for ease of organization. Have some paper clips ready in Part two to keep the student-produced material together.

Procedure

Part one

1 Students write down in pairs stages of a simple process, e.g. making tea or coffee. Give a time limit. Then invite pairs to describe a stage of the process. Note their use of marker words like *First, next* and *finally*. If they omit markers, encourage students to add these. Make a note of the ones used.

2 On the board, three columns head *Beginning, Middle* and *End*. Place one of the students' words in a column as an example. Write the other words you noted, in random order, at the side of the board. Ask students to order them correctly. Encourage peer correction.

3 Check students' understanding of the idea of a recruitment process. Explain that they are to organize the stages of such a process.

4 Give each pair a set of **Sheet one** strips, pointing out that marker words are underlined. These will help them to work out which part of the process is being described.

5 Ask students to place the strips in a logical order. Listen in, but do not intrude.

6 Now provide students with a copy of the jigsaw version (**Sheet two**). By doing the jigsaw, they will discover the order of the process. (The jigsaw reads left to right, top to bottom, like print in English.)

7 As students finish, get them to compare their strip and jigsaw versions and asking them about any differences between the two versions.

Part two: student-generated exercises

Here, pairs construct their own jigsaw.

1 Each pair agrees on a process to describe. Encourage students with business experience to choose a process from work, e.g. a production or managerial process. As students write, take notes on common errors and good use of language, particularly marker words. Encourage students to really break down the process into component parts and find 10–20 stages.

2 Students write each stage on a strip. Give them a blank sheet for this, plus scissors and a paper clip for cutting and keeping the strips together. Monitor for accuracy.

3 Give each pair a blank jigsaw (**Sheet three**). Students should transfer the segments of their process onto it, leaving blank squares where appropriate. Each process should have a title.

4 Both the strip and jigsaw sheets should be cut up and kept in sets so that they can be redistributed to other groups. The new group puts the material in order and checks it as before.

If there is a lot of interest and you have enough jigsaws, rotate the activity again and encourage further questions about the processes described.

5 When students finish, ask them to comment on whether their colleagues' processes were difficult to organize and why.

Sheet one

First a job description is prepared.

After that we accept no more applications.

This breaks the job down into its different elements.

The selection process starts by eliminating any candidates who do not have the essential requirements mentioned in the newspaper advert.

Then the job description is used to write an advert.

It proceeds by the remaining candidates being graded from 'A' to 'C'

Here, salary and conditions are included.

'A' indicates a candidate who fulfils all the advert's criteria, including the extra, 'desirable' ones, 'B' shows a good candidate and 'C' a satisfactory one.

Next, the post is advertised internally,

The third stage of selection is deciding who to interview.

– usually on the company notice board.

Generally about ten candidates are interviewed, As first, then Bs and Cs are considered.

This is because our company has a policy of using our own employees first for new jobs.

After interview, two or three candidates are shortlisted and invited to attend final interviews.

After advertising internally, if no one suitable is found,

The final interviews take place a week or so later,

we carry out the second advertising stage in the newspaper.

then, lastly, the best candidate is offered the job.

Normally, candidates have two weeks to apply.

The whole process just described usually takes from four to six weeks.

Sheet two

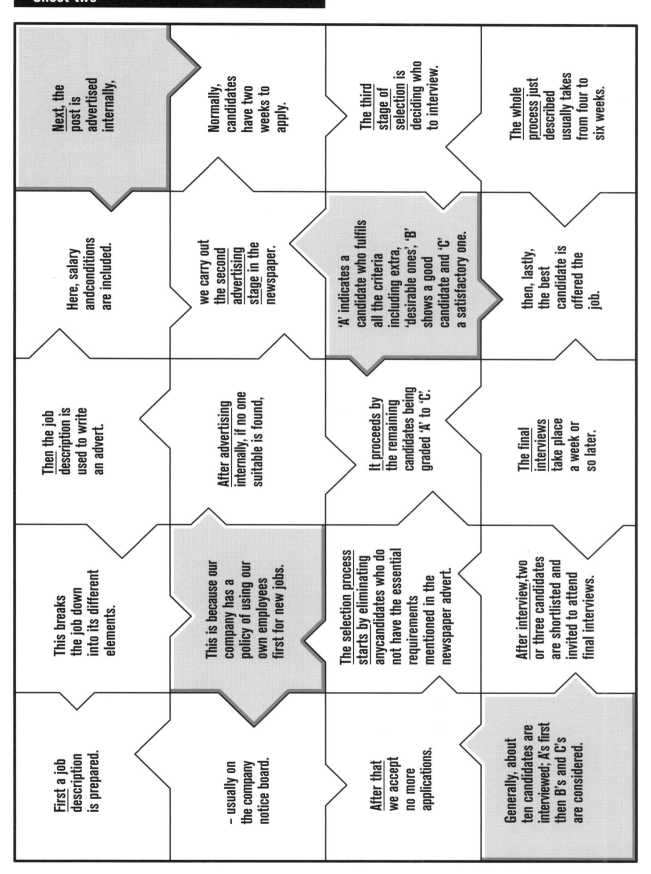

Next, the post is advertised internally,

Normally, candidates have two weeks to apply.

The third stage of selection is deciding who to interview.

The whole process just described usually takes from four to six weeks.

Here, salary andconditions are included.

we carry out the second advertising stage in the newspaper.

'A' indicates a candidate who fulfils all the criteria including extra, 'desirable ones', 'B' shows a good candidate and 'C' a satisfactory one.

then, lastly, the best candidate is offered the job.

Then the job description is used to write an advert.

After advertising internally, if no one suitable is found,

It proceeds by the remaining candidates being graded 'A' to 'C'.

The final interviews take place a week or so later.

This breaks the job down into its different elements.

This is because our company has a policy of using our own employees first for new jobs.

The selection process starts by eliminating anycandidates who do not have the essential requirements mentioned in the newspaper advert.

After interview,two or three candidates are shortlisted and invited to attend final interviews.

First a job description is prepared.

– usually on the company notice board.

After that we accept no more applications.

Generally, about ten candidates are interviewed; A's first then B's and C's are considered.

Sheet three

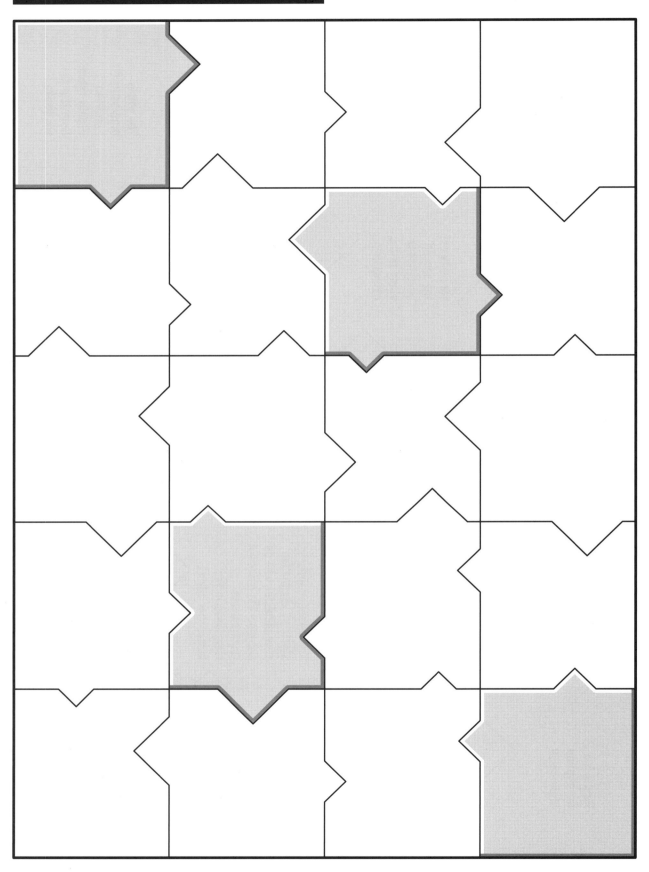

10.1 The best offer

Teaching notes

To practise Using comparative and superlative forms, e.g. *bigger, the biggest; more expensive, the most expensive;* making suggestions, e.g. *How about ... ? Why don't we ... ?;* agreeing and disagreeing, persuading and reaching a decision in a group.

Level Lower to upper-intermediate. With upper-intermediate student, omit stages one and two of the procedure.

Pre-experience learners No special requirements.

Class size Multiples of four are best. Can also be played in threes.

One-to-one Not really suitable. However, you could turn all the cards from one category face up at the same time, and ask your student to make comparisons and use the superlative form to make a choice.

Overall timing 60–80 minutes.

Potentially difficult vocabulary *double glazing, satellite TV dish, security system, balcony, liqueurs, Bingo hall, burglar alarm, smoke alarm, fitted kitchen, fish pond, terraced* and *semi-detached houses, cottage*

You will need One copy of each sheet of **Game cards** (pp100–2) per group of four (or three) students, with all the cards cut out. Clip each set of cards ('holiday', 'restaurant' and 'conference venue') together.

Procedure

1 Write the words *holiday, restaurant* and *conference venue* on the board at the top of three columns. Then write *Can be ...* underneath. Elicit adjectives from the class and put them in the columns.

2 Choose some sample adjectives from the board and elicit the comparative and superlative forms. Point out the two comparative and superlative forms (*er/est* and *more/most*) and any irregularities such as spellings, e.g. *happy – happier* and *hot – hotter.*

3 Put your class into small groups of three or four students and explain that they are going to play a game where they compare different holidays, restaurants and conference venues and decide, as a group, which one is best for them. Hand out the first set of cards to each group and ask them to place the cards face down on the table.

4 Add the following questions to the relevant the columns on the board: *Where will you go together? Where will you go together for lunch? Where will you go together?*

5 To play, students take one card each from the pile. (One card will remain if three students are playing.) They should read the information on their card. Then one student reads out one

fact from their card, e.g. 'My holiday is £500 for three weeks.' The others then add information from their cards and make comparisons with their own holidays. For example, another student could say, 'My holiday is cheaper than yours – it's only £200. But it is shorter, only two weeks.' Each student should try to persuade the others in the group that their card is the best option.

When the group has made a decision, one student makes a note of the choice and the reasons for choosing it, e.g. 'Holiday: Goa – because it's the sunniest and most unusual place'. Remind students not to show their cards to each other, otherwise this becomes a reading exercise rather than a speaking and listening one. They may, however, make notes about their group members' cards if they wish. Then give the groups the next set of cards.

6 Ask the groups to start. Move around the class, listening for good and poor usage of the target structures and make notes. Encourage any groups not using the target language to do so.

7 When everyone finishes, ask a representative from each group to describe their group's choices briefly and to justify them.

Feedback

Use your notes from stage six above to provide feedback at the end.

Note: You can adapt this material to your students' specific situation by devising cards with products or services provided by their company and competitors.

Game cards: Conference venue

CONFERENCE VENUE A

PLACE: Small seaside town.

PRICE: £100 per person per day.

FOOD: One choice of hot and cold dish at each meal.

FACILITIES: Small bar, karaoke three times a week, live entertainment once a week.

FEATURES: Beautiful view, fresh air, beach.

ACCESS: Station is 3 km away – taxis available. Bus station 1 km.

CONFERENCE VENUE B

PLACE: Big city.

PRICE: £200 per person per day.

FOOD: Large choice of menu at each meal. (At least four dishes per course.)

FACILITIES: Gym, sauna, steam room, large bar, five star restaurant, small cinema, laundry service.

FEATURES: City night life, cultural events.

ACCESS: By train, metro, bus or taxi. Airport 12 km away.

CONFERENCE VENUE C

PLACE: Mountain village ranch.

PRICE: £120 per person per day.

FOOD: Wide variety, healthy, vegetarian and vegan menu. (Four to six dishes for main course.)

FACILITIES: Massage, natural spa, horse riding, canoeing, climbing.

FEATURES: Extremely peaceful atmosphere.

ACCESS: By minibus only – can be booked with the centre.

CONFERENCE VENUE D

PLACE: Edge of town, purpose-built.

PRICE: £160 per person per day.

FOOD: Choice of three dishes at each meal.

FACILITIES: Large gym, sauna, video, bar.

FEATURES: Quiet location, efficient staff.

ACCESS: Regular shuttle bus service from the centre of the town. This is included in the price.

Game cards: Restaurant

RESTAURANT A

TYPE OF RESTAURANT: Italian pizza parlour.

POSITION: Town centre, five minutes' walk from the classroom.

PRICE: Cheap – about £8.00–£11.00 per person for two courses and a drink.

DRINKS: Mostly beer and soft drinks, a few wines and liqueurs.

CHARACTER: Noisy, busy and cheerful.

RESTAURANT B

TYPE OF RESTAURANT: French.

POSITION: On the edge of town – 25 minutes' walk or ten minutes' taxi drive away.

PRICE: Expensive – about £30.00–£35.00 per person for three courses with wine.

DRINKS: A very wide choice of wines and liqueurs.

CHARACTER: Formal and exclusive.

RESTAURANT C

TYPE OF RESTAURANT: English – part of a hotel.

POSITION: In the countryside, half an hour's drive away.

PRICE: £12.50 for the set three course lunch with a glass of wine.

DRINKS: A full bar available.

CHARACTER: Very friendly and polite service. Nice view over the hills.

RESTAURANT D

TYPE OF RESTAURANT: Indian curry house.

POSITION: Town centre – ten minutes' walk away.

PRICE: £9.00–£13.00 for three courses with no drinks.

DRINKS: Only non-alcoholic drinks served, but you can bring your own wine or beer.

CHARACTER: Quiet and intimate.

Game cards: Holiday

HOLIDAY A

LENGTH:	Three weeks.
PLACE:	Blackpool, UK.
PRICE:	£500 per person.
ACCOMMODATION:	Two-star hotel, 500 metres from the beach.
WEATHER:	Can rain a lot, even in summer.
FOOD:	All meals included in the price.
ENTERTAINMENT:	Fun fairs, ten Bingo halls, 12 cinemas plus dance halls and two theatres.
ATMOSPHERE:	Crowded, noisy and fun.

HOLIDAY B

LENGTH:	Ten days.
PLACE:	Goa, India.
PRICE:	£700 per person.
ACCOMMODATION:	Four-star hotel, 100 metres from the beach.
WEATHER:	Hot and sunny all year round.
FOOD:	Breakfast and evening meal included.
ENTERTAINMENT:	Some local festivals and barbecue parties on the beach.
ATMOSPHERE:	Peaceful, few people and beautiful scenery.

HOLIDAY C

LENGTH:	Two weeks.
PLACE:	Trekking in Nepal, Himalayas.
PRICE:	£600 per person. (Tour guide included.)
ACCOMMODATION:	In tents, camping.
WEATHER:	Cold at night and hot during the day.
FOOD:	You make your own. Local food is very cheap.
ENTERTAINMENT:	Socialize with the other people on the trip. Occasional mountain village party.
ATMOSPHERE:	Mountainous, quiet.

HOLIDAY D

LENGTH:	Two weeks.
PLACE:	Tenerife, Canary Islands.
PRICE:	£200 per person.
ACCOMMODATION:	One-star hotel in a town. Thirty minutes to the beach.
WEATHER:	Mostly very warm, but not all year round.
FOOD:	Breakfast only provided.
ENTERTAINMENT:	A lot of cafés, restaurants, night clubs and discos to go to.
ATMOSPHERE:	A busy tourist resort with a lot of young UK tourists.

10.2 Selling yourself

Teaching notes

To practise Using the comparative and superlative forms, describing oneself and preparing for an interview.

Level Pre-intermediate and intermediate.

Pre-experience learners This is not a suitable activity for such learners as it is based upon work skills analysis. However, you could consider using a different topic, such as their skills in English.

Class size Two plus. If the numbers are uneven, have one group of three.

One-to-one As long as the student is comfortable with discussing his or her work skills, this is fine.

Overall timing 30–40 minutes.

You will need One copy of the **Worksheet** (p104) per student in your class and some pairs of scissors.

Procedure

1 Lead in by explaining that students are going to practise selling themselves in an interview for promotion using their USPs (Unique Selling Points). First, though, they have to analyze their skills.

2 Demonstrate the activity yourself, putting the headings from the worksheet on the board, or using an OHP. Fill in a few items in each column as an example. Discuss a job you have done in the past or make up a character whose skills you are analyzing.

3 Now hand out the **Worksheet** and ask your students to fill it in for themselves. You may need to help students out here with vocabulary (as students might have different jobs this may be difficult to prepare beforehand).

4 Now demonstrate how comparative sentences can be made using this worksheet. Using the information you already have on the board, write one comparative and one superlative

sentence yourself. Point out the instruction at the bottom of the worksheet and ask students to write sentences for themselves. Stress the importance of being positive in interviews! Again, help out with vocabulary and check for accuracy.

5 When your students have finished, put them into pairs. Ask each student to cut off the first column of the worksheet (*Skills I need in my job*) and give it to their partner. Each student will use this strip to interview their partner. Provide the following question cues, either on the board or on an OHT: *Can you ... ? How good are you at ... (+ ing)? Which things can you do better now than when you started your job? What can you do best? What do you think is the most important skill for doing this job? Why should you get promotion?* Listen to the interviews and note any recurring problems, especially with comparative and superlative forms.

Feedback

Ask each pair to comment briefly on how their interview went. Provide feedback immediately, or next lesson, on students' comments during their interviews.

Worksheet

Skills I need in my job.	When I started I was .... at this.	Now I am .... at this.
e.g. organize files	e.g. quite good but slow	e.g. very good and quick

Write some sentences comparing your abilities now (in the third column) with what they were like when you started work.

e.g.: I am better and quicker at organizing files now.

....

....

....

....

....

....

....

....

....

What are your best points? Underline them in the sentences above.

11.1 Intonation patterns

Teaching notes

To practise Listening to and observing the effect of intonation in English.

Level All levels. The 'smileys' guide elementary learners to the meaning.

Pre-experience learners No special requirements.

Class size Two plus.

One-to-one You read the examples and discuss your student's choices afterwards. There is scope for detailed discussion of the differences in intonation between English and the student's first language.

Overall timing 20–30 minutes.

You will need One **Worksheet** (p106) per student. An optional cassette recording of you reading the words on the **Worksheet** (see stage three below).

Procedure

1 Give an example of how the meaning of a word can be affected by intonation, for example, 'Oh' can be made to sound shocked, bored or interested in scandal. Elicit some suggestions about what causes the word to sound more or less 'emotional' (e.g. change in degree of pitch, length of utterance).

2 Hand out the **Worksheets**. Ask students, working in pairs, to predict which graphs refer to sentences 1, 2 and 3. Emphasize that there are no hard and fast rules about intonation; much depends on who is speaking, and in what context. However, this activity is designed to guide students a little.

3 Tell students that they are now going to listen to you reading the sentences on the **Worksheet** with intonations as indicated (positive, negative and indifferent). As they listen, students should check their pencilled answers and if they now do not agree with those answers, they should add the new answers. It may be difficult for you to repeat your performance precisely, and so it is a good idea to record the words beforehand. Then you can simply replay the tape.

4 Pairs compare their answers again, noting and discussing any changes.

5 Check students' answers using the **Key** below and ask those students who have made alterations to share them with the class. Encourage discussion.

Key

1 A2   B1   C3

2 A2   B3   C1

3 A2   B1   C3

4 A3   B1   C2

6 Provide feedback and also ask students to offer some conclusions to the class about how pitch, range and length affect meaning. (Usually, the greater the pitch change, plus the emphasis on a word, the greater the emotion.)

Follow up

Students can try a negotiating activity, possibly using the role play material from **Someone else's shoes**, where one student tries to use as little intonation as possible, and the other student speaks expressively. Pairs could discuss the effect of the speaker who lacks intonation variation. One pair can perform to the class, encouraging a general discussion.

Worksheet

1 *Hello*

A

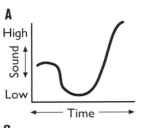

High
Sound ↕
Low
← Time →

B

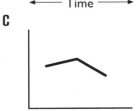

C

Meanings:

1 What a surprise and a pleasure to see you. ☐

2 What is going on? I am suspicious. ☐

3 You again. We meet ten times a day at work. ☐

3 *No*

A

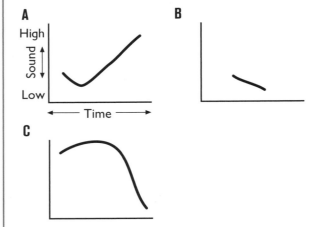

High
Sound ↕
Low
← Time →

B

C

Meanings:

1 You cannot go home early. No discussion! ☐

2 I hadn't heard that. It's new to me. ☐

3 It's not possible, surely! ☐

2 *Yes*

A

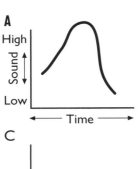

High
Sound ↕
Low
← Time →

C

Meanings:

1 I don't really agree with you. ☐

2 I've got that job I really wanted. ☐

3 Oh no, not someone else coming to interrupt me – but I must be polite. ☐

B

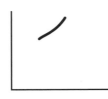

4 *Really?*

A

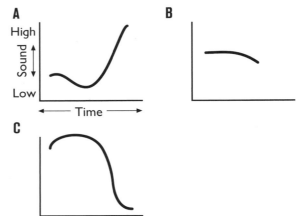

High
Sound ↕
Low
← Time →

B

C

Meanings:

1 Do you have to keep talking in such a boring way? ☐

2 That's disgusting! How can you be so rude?! ☐

3 That's amazing. You surprize me. ☐

11.2 A phonemic phone call

Teaching notes

To practise Recognizing the phonemic symbols and organizing a business telephone call into the correct order.

Level Intermediate.

Pre-experience learners No special preparation needed.

Class size Two plus. This activity can be done with a large class.**

One-to-one This is possible if the teacher takes the role of the other half of the pair.

Overall timing 20–30 minutes.

You will need Smaller class option*: One cut up version of the **Worksheet** (p108) per pair with A and B strips in two sets, mixed up; or if you are using the large class option below,** one cut up version for the class.

Students need to be familiar with The phonemic symbols for English sounds. These are available with a key in any good monolingual English dictionary. This activity is a good follow up to drilling the sounds and symbols or for revising them later.

Procedure

1 Smaller class option*: Divide the class in half. Give one half a complete set of **Speaker A** strips (one set per student, mixed up). Give the remainder of the class the strips for **Speaker B**, again one set per student, mixed up. Students with **Speaker A's** strips should help each other to put the strips into a logical order, likewise students with **Speaker B's** strips. They should note possible responses from the other speaker on a sheet of paper. Dissuade students firmly from writing in normal script on their strips, as the idea of the activity is that they should read and get used to the phonemic script.

2 A and B students now pair up and sit opposite each other to check if their ordering of strips will produce a likely dialogue. They should do this by reading aloud, in turn, their respective strips. A students should start. Where necessary, the order should be negotiated and adjusted. Provide help where needed.

During stages one and two, note any symbols or sounds which give particular problems.

3 When the pairs have decided a satisfactory order, they should place their strips together as one dialogue and listen to you, with a volunteer student if possible, reading the dialogue aloud.

4 Provide feedback on any problem sounds or phonemic symbols during stages one and two.

**Large class option: Have the strips in order and hand out one strip each to random students. Keep any remaining strips yourself. Ask students to read their strips aloud to each other and try to form a line. The person who has the first strip (i.e. the beginning of the dialogue) should be at the front and the others in order. Allow students to organize themselves as far as possible. Only help where there are serious problems interpreting the phonemic symbols. Once the text is in the right order, read the remainder of the dialogue yourself.

Key

A: Brown's carpets. Good morning.
B: Good morning. Can I speak to Ms Brown please?
A: I'm sorry, she's in a meeting. Who's calling please?
B: It's John Davis from London here.
A: Right, Mr Davis. Can I take a message?
B: Er ... OK. Can you ask her to call me today?
A: Yes, of course. She has your number, doesn't she?
B: I think so, but I'll give it to you just in case.
A: Right. I've got a pen ready. Go ahead.

B: It's 0171-336-9842.
A: Can you repeat that please? The line is bad.
B: Yes, sorry. 0171-336-9842. Did you get it that time?
A: Yes, thank you. I'll pass on the message once Ms Brown finishes her meeting.
B: Thanks and could you tell her that it's about the Italian order?
A: Yes of course. Goodbye Mr Davis.
B: Bye – and thanks.

Worksheet

A braʊnz kaːpɪts gʊd mɔːnɪŋ

B gʊd mɔːnɪŋ kan aɪ spiːk tə mɔz braʊn pliːz

A aɪm sɒriː ʃɪːz ɪn ə miːtɪŋ huːz kɔːlɪŋ pliːz

B ɪts dʒɒn deɪːvɪs frɒm lʌndən hɪ

A raɪt mɪstə deɪːvɪs kən aɪ tɪkə mə sɪdʒ?

B ɜː ... ʊ keɪ kən juː aːsk hɜː tuː kɔːl miːt deɪ

A yesə v kɔːs ʃɪː hæz jɔːɪ mbə dʌʒ nt ʃɪː?

B aɪ θɪŋk sʊ bʌt aɪl gɪv ɪt tə juː dʌvzst ɪn keɪs

A raɪt aɪv gɒtə pen rediː g ʊə hed

B ɪtsə ʊ wɒn seɪ n wɒn dʌ bʌ l θriː sɪks naɪn eɪt fɔː tuː

A kən juː rɪpiːt θæt pliːz? ðə laɪn ɪz bæd

B yes, sə riː ʊ wɒn seɪ n wɒn dʌ bʌ l θriː sɪks naɪn eɪt fɔː tuː dɪd juː get ɪt ðæt taɪm?

A yes θænkju aɪl paːs ɒn ðə mesɪdʒ wɒns mə z braʊn fɪnɪʃɪz hɜː miːtɪŋ

B θænks ən kʊd juː tel hɜː ðæt ɪtsə baʊt ðiː ɪtælɪ nʌːdʒ?

A yesə v kɔːs gʊdbaɪ mɪstə deɪːvɪs

B baɪ n θænks

11.3 Strong or weak?

Teaching notes

To practise Recognizing how strong and weak vowel sounds are used, in the context of a description of a process.

Level Intermediate and above.

Pre-experience learners No special requirements.

Class size Multiples of three are ideal but you can give sections 1 and 2 of **Sheet A** (p110) together with different numbers.

One-to-one Yes. Work on **Sheet A** together.

Overall timing 45 minutes.

Potentially difficult vocabulary *crucial, means* (n), *financial backing, feasibility, launch* (these words are in italics in the text).

You will need One copy of **Sheet A**, cut into three, for every three students and one copy of **Sheet B** (p111) per student.

Students need to be familiar with The phonemic symbols for English or at least those for the single vowels.

Procedure

1 Present weak forms using the following example if you wish:

Would you like a copy of the report?

Ask students to mark the stressed words (*like*, *copy*, *report*) and then elicit which words have the 'lazy' schwa sound (*you*, *a*, *of* and *the*) and why, if possible.

2 Small class option: give each student a different part of **Sheet A**. If you have six or more in a class, pairs can work together on the same exercise. Give help where necessary and make sure that they have the correct answer before going on to stage three. (See **Key**.)

3 Give each student or pair **Sheet B**. They complete the gaps with the appropriate word(s) from **Sheet A**.

4 Each student now joins up with two other students who had the other sections of **Sheet A**. They should form a group of three. They then fill in and check their **Sheet Bs** together.

5 Now students read the text aloud. Using **Sheet A** to help them, they should mark the gap-fill words with a schwa symbol, ǝ / or the symbol for the longer sound as appropriate.

6 Ask a student to read the text fairly slowly. Check students' answers regularly using an OHT if possible, and revealing each section after it has been read aloud.

Follow up

1 Students focus on the use of *the* in the text. (This is particularly useful for monolingual groups whose first language does not have articles.)

2 If students are keen, they could identify all the weak forms in the text (*of*, *as*, *of*, etc.).

3 Students find all the marker words for describing a process. (See **Key, p112**.)

Sheet A

1 *to*

Mark the stressed words in each sentence, as shown in the example:

   /   /   /   /   /

I went to my bank to try to get a loan but they refused!

a) We want to extend our product range.

b) Do you have access to your personal file?

c) He's trying to improve efficiency.

Read each sentence aloud. What sound does *to* have in each case?

Now complete this rule about the pronunciation of *to*. Normally *to* is pronounced /t / except when the word following it starts with a ....

----

2 *for*

Mark the stressed words in each sentence as shown in the example:

   /   /   /   /   /

Are you for or against this proposal?

a) I am waiting for a reply from our agent.

b) Time for coffee!

Read each sentence aloud. What sound does *for* have in each case?

Now complete the rule about the pronunciation of *for*.

Normally *for* is pronounced /f / except when it is ....
Then it has the sound / /.

----

3 *the*

Read the following sentences aloud. Which sound does *the* have in each case – /ðiː/ or /ð /?

a) I don't like the idea of redundancies.

b) That's the last time I work late this month!

c) Why didn't you come to the opening of the new building?

d) It's not just a new product, it's the new product on the market!

e) It's not the meeting itself I fear, it's the aftermath.

Complete this rule: *the* is pronounced /ðiː/ when it comes before a word starting with a .... or when the speaker wants to .... the word for some reason. Otherwise it is pronounced / /.

Sheet B

Here a bank employee working in the special advisory unit for small business owners, talks about what happens when a new client comes to them for help. Complete the gaps with the appropriate word or words from Sheet A.

'.......................... first stage of .... process is .... someone

.... approach us with an idea .... starting their business. At

this stage we don't ask .... any detailed plans or documentation as we

like .... keep it fairly informal.

'Next, one of my unit's advisors looks at .... idea and puts down any

questions they have. They then arrange .... meet .... person

concerned .... a preliminary discussion and ask ....

questions they have, as well as responding .... any which ....

client has.

'After this meeting, our manager liaises with a senior manager about

.... *feasibility* of .... new business. What's *crucial* is usually

whether there's a market .... new product or service and

also whether .... client has the security and *means* ....

convince us .... provide financial support. If there is, we usually give

.... go-ahead .... next stage which is

.... client .... write a business plan. We send

detailed material .... help .... client write ....

plan.

'Once .... plan is written, we usually go through it with ....

client, paying particular attention .... "predicted costs"

section of it as people are often rather unrealistic about these!

'The plan is considered by a group of senior bankers and if our client's application is successful, we not only provide *financial backing*, but also a full range of services and advice as they *launch* their new venture and as it develops. All in all I think that we offer a very practical and useful service.'

Key

Sheet A

1   /   /   /

  a) We want to extend our product range.

              /   /   /

  b) Do you have access to your personal file?

          /   /   /

  c) He's trying to improve efficiency.

  Normally *to* is pronounced /ʧə / except when the word following it starts with a **vowel**.

2   /   /   /

  a) I am waiting for a reply from our agent.

      /   /

  b) Time for coffee!

  Normally *for* is pronounced /fə / except when it is **emphasized**. Then it has the sound /fə :/.

3

  /ðiː/ in a), c) and the first 'the' in d).

  /ðə / in b) and the second 'the' in d).

  The is pronounced /ðiː/ when it comes before a word starting with a **vowel** or when the speaker wants to **emphasize** the word for some reason. Otherwise it is pronounced /ðə /.

Sheet B

'<u>The</u> first stage of <u>the</u> process is <u>for</u> someone <u>to</u> approach us with an idea <u>for</u> starting their business. At this stage we don't ask <u>for</u> any detailed plans or documentation as we like to keep it fairly informal.

'Next, one of my unit's advisors looks at *<u>the</u> idea and puts down any questions they have. They then arrange <u>to</u> meet <u>the</u> person concerned <u>for</u> a preliminary discussion, and ask <u>the</u> questions they have, as well as responding *<u>to</u> any which <u>the</u> client has.

'After this meeting, our manager liaises with a senior manager about <u>the</u> *feasibility* of <u>the</u> new business. What's *crucial* is usually whether there's a market <u>for</u> <u>the</u> new product or service and also whether <u>the</u> client has the security and means <u>to</u> convince us <u>to</u> provide financial support. If there is, we usually give <u>the</u> go ahead <u>for</u> <u>the</u> next stage which is <u>for</u> <u>the</u> client *to* write a business plan. We send detailed material <u>to</u> help *the* client <u>to</u> write the business plan.

'Once <u>the</u> plan is written, we usually go through it with <u>the</u> client, paying particular attention to <u>the</u> "predicted costs" section of it as people are often rather unrealistic about these!

'The plan is considered by a group of senior bankers and if our client's application is successful, we not only provide *financial backing*, but also a full range of services and advice as they *launch* their new venture and as it develops. All in all I think that we offer a very practical and useful service.'

Pronunciation note: Apart from the words with * before them, all the <u>underlined</u> (inserted) words are weak forms with *the* /ə / at the end. The two exceptions are followed by words starting with vowels so *the = /ðiː/ and *to = /tuː/.

12.1 A memo to your students

Teaching notes

To provide Constructive written feedback on your students' oral work.

Level Any.

Pre-experience learners No special requirements.

Class size Any.

One-to-one Yes. It can be useful as a way of commenting on your student's presentation or speech.

Overall timing Average 15–20 minutes, depending on the number of examples on your memo and the speed of your students' response to them.

Procedure

1 Prior to a lesson which is to contain free practice oral work, prepare a sheet for yourself divided into two, marked + and ?.

2 During the lesson, or using a recording of it, note good and poor use of language. (The sample memo was produced after a lesson on the language of meetings, so agreeing/disagreeing, querying and making suggestions were focused on.)

3 Organize your notes to produce your own memo. There is a blank memo **Worksheet** (p114) for you to use if you wish. Remember to:
   i) use clear, businesslike presentation; word process or type where possible
   ii) make sure that there are some positive observations and put these first
   iii) try to provide utterances from as many students as possible; do not name individual students, as it can be embarrassing or demotivating for those concerned
   iv) similarly, avoid naming those who have made errors.

4 At the next lesson, hand out the memo, or, if all the students work in the same company, send it through the internal mail service beforehand. When you come to discuss the 'Expressions which could be improved' section, allow students to compare each other's ideas before you comment. You can get plenty of useful information at this stage and sometimes students will work out everything for themselves.

Remember that there are often several valid ways of rewriting a sentence or phrase. Discourage the students from expecting the 'right' answer from you.

Worksheet

Example memo to your students

MEMORANDUM

To: All members of the Business English class

From: Jane Cordell   **Date:** 1.4.1999

Re: Last lesson's practice meeting

Present: Agnieszka (chairperson), Ahmed, Sin Jong,
Anna, Ziad, Jane (minutes)

Comment:

Thanks to Agnieszka for being a firm and fair chairperson who made sure that everyone had a chance to speak.

Here are some examples of good phrases used during the meeting:

'Can I interrupt here, please?'

'If we were to spend so much money on a printer we would have nothing left to improve the office.'

'I agree with you completely.'

'Don't you think that we should listen to everyone's opinion?'

'I'm sorry, I can't agree with you.'

These phrases are incorrect. See if you can correct them.

'I would propose the coffee cups.'

'I am not agree.'

'We shouldn't choose neither the painting or the printer; they're too expensive.'

'How can we make business in such an office?'

'Have we an information about this?'

THANK YOU ALL FOR PARTICIPATING WELL.

Worksheet

Example at top of first sheet

MEMORANDUM

To:

From: **Date:**

Re:

Thank you for your participation in last lesson's discussion. Congratulations on the examples of good language below. See if you can correct the phrases in the second section.

Good language used:

Expressions which could be improved:

12.2 Pairs to compare

Teaching notes

To practise Recognition of errors and self-correction.

Level Any, as you use your students' work.

Pre-experience learners No special requirements.

Class size Any.

One-to-one Yes. This can be a good starting point for discussion of the student's errors.

Overall timing 10–20 minutes, depending on the number of sentences included and amount of discussion generated.

You will need Your own sheet such as the sample one below, containing varied examples of errors taken from your students' written work, paired up with correct examples. (You can use material from oral work, but be careful not to inhibit particularly shy students from developing fluency.) Try to choose errors which are representative of your students. For lower levels in particular, it is best to include only one error per sentence. If you include more than one error per sentence for higher levels, indicate this clearly, as below. Copy one sheet per student or put the sentences on an OHT.

Procedure

1 Tell your students that you have put together a set of sentences from their work and that they are going to practise the useful skills of recognizing and correcting errors.

2 Give students one worksheet between two to encourage pairwork, or reveal the OHT, also asking for students to work in pairs. Students decide which sentence is correct in each case. Listen in to their discussions. Make sure each student has a worksheet before giving feedback.

3 Give feedback, but avoid simply telling students the correct answers if you can. Encourage inter-pair discussion. (If you have a large class, pairs can team up to compare their answers before feedback.) Remember to have clear explanations ready of why each sentence is right or wrong.

Samples

Choose the correct answer from each pair, **a** or **b**.

1 a) He is working for my company since 1989.

   b) He has been working for my company since 1989.

2 a) I normally go to work at 8.15.

   b) I normally go to the work at 8.15.

Note: There are TWO mistakes in sentence 3 below.

3 a) The conference it was very marvellous.

   b) The conference was absolutely marvellous.

4 a) Everybody works very hard here, don't they?

   b) Every body work very hard here, doesn't he?

13.1 When it goes wrong

Teaching notes

To practise Giving advice, writing in English, modals.

Level Elementary and pre-intermediate.

Pre-experience learners These learners will not have business problems to comment on but could write about other difficulties that they have, e.g. with their studies, their accommodation, etc.

Class size Works best with three or more students.

One-to-one This is really a group activity.

Overall timing 45 minutes.

You will need To ensure that all students have blank paper and pens.

Procedure

1 Tell students about a real or imagined dilemma which you have and ask them for their advice. As they reply, write the phrases which they use for giving advice on the board. If you expect students to know more phrases than are on the board, try to elicit them, otherwise provide them. Keep the phrases on the board during the activity as a reminder.

2 Each student needs a blank sheet of paper with their name at the top. They should then have a few moments' silence to think about any problem that they have at work. Afterwards they should describe the problem on paper. Circulate and help out with accuracy and vocabulary problems.

3 Students then hand their sheet on to the next person and that person reads it and writes their advice on the same sheet. Again, monitor the writing and help out if necessary.

4 This process continues until everyone has added their advice to the sheets and the author receives her/his sheet back. (In very large groups, this may not be practical, so split the group into smaller ones for this purpose.)

5 When students have had a chance to read the advice, get feedback from each about the best piece of advice they received, and what they think of the reaction to their problem.

Note: In some cultures it may not be appropriate to ask students to describe their work difficulties, especially if all or many students in a class work for the same company. In this case it would be a good idea for you to assign students an imaginary business person's role. Ask them to think up a problem which that person might have. It can be fun to choose famous people for this activity.

13.2 Business scruples

Teaching notes

To practise Giving advice using the second conditional form, e.g. *If I were you, I would ...* and expressing opinion, e.g. *I think you should try doing X because ...* /*I think she was wrong to do Y because ...*

Level Mid-intermediate plus.

Pre-experience learners This activity presents moral dilemmas in the business world. Before you start you might like to get your pre-experience learners to predict what these dilemmas might be.

Class size Two plus. The game can be played in threes or fours.

One-to-one You can use this activity easily with one student. Alternate the roles of advisor and the person seeking advice.

Overall timing 40–65 minutes.

Potentially difficult vocabulary *fiddling the expenses, to be distracted, a bribe* (see **Glossary** after cards). Also: *petty cash, promotion* and *hint* (v)

You will need A set of prepared **Game cards** (p119), per group of three or four students in your class. Optional: You can distribute one copy per group of the **Glossary** if needed.

Students need to be familiar with A range of expressions for giving advice and their pronunciation and stress in context, e.g. 'It'd be a good idea if you told him,' 'If I were you, I'd ...' 'I think you should probably ... '

Procedure

1 Group your students in threes or fours and hand out one set of cards to each group.

2 Explain that they take it in turns to pick up a card and read out a problem situation. The other members of the group should then give advice. The cardholder decides whose advice to take (if any). Demonstrate this procedure with one card in one group.

3 Use your discretion about how many cards to give to students. Ten are provided, but this

may be too many for groups who are likely to be able to discuss each point at length. As students play the game, observe and make notes on their use of the expressions for giving advice.

4 Usually the game generates a lot of discussion. Round it off when the groups have finished by asking which situation was the most difficult to solve and why.

Feedback

From your notes made in stage three above provide oral comments or later, written ones.

Game cards

Just before leaving the office, I saw a colleague whom I like very much taking money out of the petty cash box. No one else was around and he did not see me.

What should I do now?

I've discovered accidentally that a colleague has been fiddling her expense forms to get herself more money than she should.

Should I do anything about this? What should I do?

My boss has been paying me a lot of attention recently and today invited me out for an evening meal, hinting that if I go, promotion may be possible. S/he is a good boss. I want promotion and I want to keep on good terms with her/him, but I am worried that s/he wants to have a romantic relationship with me.

What should I do about the dinner invitation?

My best friend at work has been complaining that her husband doesn't seem to be at home very much these days. Yesterday evening I saw her husband with an attractive woman entering a hotel. It could have been a customer I suppose.

Do I say anything? If so, what?

I found out that a junior employee who reports to me has been using the office phone to call his friends in New Zealand.

How do I deal with this situation?

I am head of a department of 11 employees. My director says that due to cuts, I must reduce the department to ten.

How do I decide who will go? And how do I arrange for the person to be told the bad news?

One of my assistants comes into work about half an hour late every day. S/he works very hard once s/he arrives, but you notice that the other people in the office are starting to resent the situation.

What do you do?

I am in a job which is secure and well-paid but which I find boring. I have been offered a more interesting job by another company but it's not as well-paid as the one I have now and is only a two-year contract to start with.

Do I change?

One evening, working late, I went into another office to get a file I needed. I was shocked to see two of the firm's senior financial controllers apparently changing the figures for the company on the computer. They were surprised to see me and immediately offered a bribe of 5% of the money they expect to make if I keep quiet.

What should I say and do?

I have only been working for my company for four months. I found it hard to get a job and enjoy the work I am doing now. The union has called a strike of all workers in my company to protest at this year's low pay rise. The bosses are angry about this. I do not want to be unpopular with the bosses or colleagues.

Do I strike?

Glossary

Fiddling the expense forms: telling lies about how much money you spent on official business/claiming more than you should get.

Bribe: money offered to do something illegal or corrupt or not to report another person's illegal activities.

Distracted: unable to concentrate, thinking about other things than work.

14.1 Number noughts and crosses

Teaching notes

To practise Saying a variety of numbers and measurements.

Level Mid-intermediate and above using the version provided, but very easily adapted for lower levels.

Pre-experience learners No special business experience is required to do this activity.

Class size Two or more. Even numbers work best as it is a two team game.

One-to-one Your student could play the game against themselves. Each time they say a number correctly, their symbol (e.g. nought) is entered in the box, but for every incorrect number the other symbol is entered.

Overall timing This depends partly on level, but approximately 20–25 minutes.

You will need A board and chalk/marker plus your own copy of the game.

Students need to be familiar with Saying the type of numbers shown on the sheet.

Procedure

1 Draw the noughts and crosses grid (p121) on the board without the numbers.

2 Divide the class into two teams. Ask them if they ever play noughts and crosses, or *Tic Tac Toe* in American English. Draw the standard three by three grid on the board and put in a couple of noughts and crosses to illustrate.

3 If possible, get a student to explain the principle of the game. Now point out that the version students will play is different in two ways. First, the grid is bigger. The grid is five by five, and each team is aiming to get a continuous line of three or more squares with their symbol in it. The line can be horizontal, diagonal or vertical. If a line of three is completed, that team scores three points; a line of four, four points; and a line of five, five points. The second difference is that to get your symbol in the square, you have to pronounce a given number correctly.

4 Divide students into teams ('noughts' and 'crosses'). Toss a coin to see which team starts. They choose a square on the grid and you write the number they should say on the board, either in the square, if you have room, or next to the grid if not. Encourage the team to discuss their answer before declaring it to the class. If it is correct, their chosen symbol goes in the square. If not, the symbol of the other team goes in. This is motivating! If necessary, give a time limit for answering. Discuss errors as you go along, encouraging students to correct them.

5 In the original game, the winner is the first person to get a line of their symbols. However, in order to use the whole grid, you could award points for each line a team gets, so the winner is the team with the most points at the end.

Feedback

While the students are playing, make a note of the types of number which they found difficult and go over these at the end or next lesson.

Note: The grid format can also be used to test spelling and pronunciation of words.

	A	B	C	D	E
1	1,001	0171–624–7780 (tel. no)	$\frac{3}{4}$	24 × 33 mm	14.64 kg
2	4,227,932	95 °c	670 DM	$56.50	212 km/h
3	£16K pa	$1.4 m	31,409	+33–49–272224 (tel. no.)	18.45 (time)
4	60 cm³	7.89%	98.97%	$1\frac{2}{3}$	03.10.2004 (date)
5	12.12.1642	4:1 (ratio)	23.58 (time)	34 m²	486 − 42 = 444

14.2 Checking the details

Teaching notes

To practise Saying a variety of numbers; listening to and checking numbers; contrastive or 'correcting' stress.

Level Pre-intermediate and above.

Pre-experience learners Assuming that the vocabulary and numerical terms listed below are familiar, this should not present special problems.

Class size An even number, if you do the activity in pairs; but if it is done as a teacher-led activity, this is not important.

One-to-one Yes, this works well.

Potentially difficult vocabulary *fixed rate of interest, mortgage, profile, deputy, per* (as in 'price per metre'), *estate agent*

Overall timing 15–25 minutes, depending on class level and format chosen.

You will need One copy of the **Role play cards** (p123) per pair of students in your class if you choose to do the activity in pairs. Cut each sheet into four, as indicated. If you lead the activity, one copy of the B roles for each student and one copy of the A roles for you.

Students need to be familiar with Saying and pronouncing correctly large numbers, amounts of money, dates, including years, times (in 24-hour clock and 12-hour clock), percentages, decimals and fractions. Asking questions and checking information.

Procedure

1 Pairwork activity: Tell the class that they are going to do a role play with a partner that will involve them checking a lot of different numbers. Elicit some phrases with which students could check details (e.g. *Did you say ... ? Was that three or four thousand please?*) Also, use the following example on the board or the OHP to show how contrastive stress can be used to emphasize the correct answer:

'Is your train at 12.14?'
'No, it's at 12.40.'

This idea can also be reinforced by asking students about today's date, the time, the time the lesson started, etc. For example, you could ask: *Is it the twenty-first of June today?* and encourage *No, it's the twenty-second*, stressing the number that is different.

2 Put the class into pairs and ask students to position themselves opposite each other (to avoid the temptation to look at each other's **Role play cards**). Explain that one of them will be checking a set of figures that s/he has taken down by phone and the other person will be correcting her/him where necessary. Hand out the first **Role play cards** to the pairs. Circulate, checking that students understand what they have to do. Once the

role play starts, make notes particularly on the pronunciation of numbers and how stress is used.

3 As pairs finish, ask them to compare As' figures and Bs' corrected version. Discuss any differences and why they have occurred. Then hand the pair the second role play, getting the students to swap roles, so that the student who was correcting is now checking, and vice versa.

4 When both role plays have finished, provide feedback from your notes, remembering to praise as well as constructively criticize. Where possible, present errors and ask students to correct them themselves.

5 Teacher-led activity: Introduce the activity in the same way as in stage one above, but tell the students that they are going to correct you. The procedure is similar, except that all students are given the **Role play card** A and should shout out as soon as they notice an error in what you are saying. If your class enjoys competitive activities, you could put them into two teams and award a mark to the team that is the first to correct each number accurately.

Role play cards

ROLE PLAY 1   PERSON A

You are an estate agent; person B is a business person. They want to buy a larger set of offices for their business. Below is all the correct information on the offices. Make sure that your customer has all the right details. Correct politely where necessary.

Area of office: 8,250 m^2

Price per square metre: $17.35

Fixed interest rate mortgage for five years: 7.14%

Total cost of office (without interest): $143,137.50

Meeting to see the offices arranged for 6 February at 2.50 pm.

ROLE PLAY 1   PERSON B

You are a business person; person A is an estate agent. You want to buy a larger set of offices for your business. Your colleague wrote down some rough information about one place that the estate agent had found. Check that all the details are right and make changes where necessary.

Area of office: 8,000 m^2

Price per square metre: $15.25

Fixed interest rate mortgage for four years: 7.4%

Total cost of office (without interest): $134,247.55

Meeting to see the offices arranged for 2.15 pm on Thursday 16 February.

ROLE PLAY 2   PERSON A

You are a highly successful business person. Person B is a journalist who has come to interview you. Below are some facts about you. Make sure the journalist has all her/his facts right. Correct politely where necessary.

Annual salary: £651,348

Bonus: up to 33% of salary.

Number of employees: 4,015.

Proportion of women working for the company: one in six.

Profit last year: £14.6 million

Joined the company in 1990 as marketing director.

Became a deputy director in 1995.

Became managing director in 1998.

Born: 28.3.1955.

ROLE PLAY 2   PERSON B

You are a journalist. Person A is a highly successful business person. You are going to interview them. You already have some information about them. Make sure that it is all correct. Write in any changes which are necessary.

Annual salary: £601,238

Bonus: up to 23% of salary.

Number of employees: 4,050.

Proportion of women working for the company: one in 60.

Profit last year: £46 million

Joined the company in 1993 as marketing director.

Became a deputy director in 1995.

Became managing director in 1996.

Born: 26.3.1945.

14.3 Shared number dictations

Teaching notes

To practise Saying, listening to and writing a range of numbers.

Level Intermediate and above.

Pre-experience learners No special requirements.

Class size Any even number, as this is a pairs activity. If you have an odd number, join in.

One-to-one Yes.

Potentially difficult vocabulary *blade, foreman, compound, dimensions, pivot, spin, diameter, raw materials*

You will need Enough copies of both **Worksheets** (p125–6) for each pair of students in your class.

Students need to be familiar with Pronouncing a wide range of numbers. You may need to check that the types of numbers used have been covered before.

Procedure

1 Pair up students as A and B, and give each one A and B copies of the **Worksheet**. Explain to students that, working in pairs, they are going to read aloud a story which contains many different numbers, but some of those numbers will be missing from their sheets. They should not show each other their sheets.

2 Student A starts reading her/his worksheet and when s/he comes to a space, s/he should let Student B continues and student A write down the number s/he says. Both students should insert the missing information as they go along and take care to check that what they write is accurate, asking the other student to repeat if necessary. While the students work together, monitor the activity and note any recurring errors.

3 Only when the students have reached the end of the story should they compare each other's copies and check that they wrote down the correct numbers. Then they discuss their answers to the question at the bottom of the sheet.

4 When pairs have finished, ask them for their answers to the questions at the bottom of the sheet. The product is a turbine rotor. (You could encourage technically-minded students to draft an illustration of the product.)

5 Give feedback, discussing the problem areas you noted while students were doing the activity.

Follow up

Make a new version of the **Worksheet(s)** from the teacher's master copy, removing all the prepositions. After pairs have checked their answers, ask a student to read aloud one or two sentences. Encourage peer checking of number pronunciation as well as the prepositions. This is good revision.

Worksheet – Student A

The visitor looked at the object. It was big, made of metal, circular and consisted of lots of blades. He asked the company representative who was showing him around to explain the product to him in detail.

She said, 'Well, this product is made of steel. Its diameter is .... and it has a surface area of 2.2 m^2. It is .... thick and is made up of 56 blades which have the dimensions: .... They are attached to a central pivot which has a radius of 5 cm.

'When operating, the product spins at a speed of .... and produces 4,000 kilowatts of energy. It weighs 600 kg.'

The visitor asked about delivery and the representative answered: 'We can normally deliver within 90 days of a customer placing an order. For products with a diameter of more than .... it can take longer.'

'How much does one cost?' asked the visitor.

'Oh, quite a lot, as it involves precision work; around £10, 000 for one like this.'

'And when would I have to pay if I wanted to buy one?'

'Well, you would have to pay .... immediately to cover the cost of raw materials, and then the remaining amount by the delivery date.'

The visitor was impressed and said that he had found the visit very interesting. As he was travelling home, he realized that he had got all that information and had still not asked the name of the product.

Can you guess what the product was?

Worksheet – Student B

The visitor looked at the object. It was big, made of metal, circular and consisted of lots of blades. He asked the company representative who was showing him around to explain the product to him in detail.

She said, 'Well, this product is made of steel. Its diameter is 1.5 m and it has a surface area of .... It is 4.3 cm thick and is made up of .... blades which have the dimensions: 70 × 30 × 4.3 cm. They are attached to a central pivot which has a radius of ....

'When operating, the product spins at a speed of 200 km per hour and produces .... of energy. It weighs 600 kg.'

The visitor asked about delivery and the representative answered: 'We can normally deliver within .... days of a customer placing an order. For products with a diameter of more than 1.7 m it can take longer.'

'How much does one cost?' asked the visitor.

'Oh, quite a lot, as it involves precision work; around .... for one like this.'

'And when would I have to pay if I wanted to buy one?'

'Well, you would have to pay 40% immediately to cover the cost of raw materials, and then the remaining amount by the delivery date.'

The visitor was impressed and said that he had found the visit very interesting. As he was travelling home, he realized that he had got all that information and had still not asked the name of the product.

Can you guess what the product was?

Key

The figures the students had to ask each other for are in bold.

The visitor looked at the object. It was big, made of metal, circular and consisted of lots of blades. He asked the company representative who was showing him around to explain the product to him in detail.

She said, 'Well, this product is made of steel. Its diameter is **1.5 m** (one point five metres) and it has a surface area of **2.2 m²** (two point two square metres). It is **4.3 cm** (four point three centimetres) thick and is made up of **56** blades which have the dimensions: **70 × 30 × 4.3 cm** (seventy by thirty by four point three centimetres). They are attached to a central pivot which has a radius of **5 cm**.

'When operating, the product spins at a speed of **200 km** per hour and produces **4,000** kilowatts of energy. It weighs 600 kg.'

The visitor asked about delivery and the representative answered: 'We can normally deliver within **90** days of a customer placing an order. For products with a diameter of more than **1.7 m** (one point seven metres) it can take longer.'

'How much does one cost?' asked the visitor.

'Oh, quite a lot, as it involves precision work; around **£10,000** (ten thousand pounds) for one like this.'

'And when would I have to pay if I wanted to buy one?'

'Well, you would have to pay **40%** (forty per cent) immediately to cover the cost of raw materials, and then the remaining amount by the delivery date.'

The visitor was impressed and said that he had found the visit very interesting. As he was travelling home, he realized that he had got all that information and had still not asked the name of the product.

14.4 Testing each other

Teaching notes

To practise Forming questions about, and saying a variety of terms using numbers.

Level Pre-intermediate and above.

Pre-experience learners No special problems.

Class size Two or more.

One-to-one This is not suitable, as the game is based on the idea of students testing each other as equals.

Overall timing If the suggested ten items are used, 30-40 minutes depending on the level of the class. You can shorten or lengthen the activity by reducing or increasing the number of test items.

You will need A list of ten numerical items which students have encountered before, but which contain some challenges, e.g. dates, dimensions, weight and measurements.

Procedure

Preparation: Write out two different lists of the ten numerical items you want to test. Put the items in a different order on each list so you do not repeat each type of number immediately when playing the game.

1 Divide the class into two teams. Tell them that they are going to prepare a test about saying numbers for the other team.

2 Give each team one list and explain that they have to write questions for the answers, i.e. numbers, on the list. They must avoid saying the exact number at all costs. For lower levels, it will be especially helpful if you give an example or two. So if the answer is 777, the question could be *What do you get when you take 223 from 1,000? Or for a set of dimensions: How would you describe a cupboard you wanted a carpenter to make for you with a depth of 90 cm, a length of 1 m and width 1 m 30 – how would you describe the dimensions correctly?* Encourage the

team to use their imagination when writing the questions and monitor their questions for accuracy before starting the test.

3 Begin when both teams have a set of accurate questions that avoid telling the other team the answer. One team reads their first question aloud and the other writes it down and discusses the answer together. You can give a time limit. The team who asked the question tells the answering team whether their answer was correct or not. If it was, the answering team scores a point on the board. If not, the questioning team scores a point. As the class runs this activity, note the type of questions that students are having difficulty with.

4 In the case of a draw, give one last tie breaker question. The first team to answer correctly wins.

Feedback

In a future lesson, go over the types of numbers that you observed students had difficulty with.

Note: The same game can be used to test and revise vocabulary items, with the teams writing definitions of words.